Camping Together as Christians

A GUIDE FOR JUNIOR HIGH CAMP LEADERS

by John and Ruth Ensign

Illustrated by Ruth Singley Ensign

Published for the Cooperative Publication Association

JOHN KNOX PRESS
Richmond, Virginia

To our parents
and
To our own little campers
Jacqueline Susan
Martha Anne
and
Stephen Dewees

Library of Congress Catalog Card Number: 58-6252
Copyright © 1958 by C. D. Deans, Richmond, Virginia
Printed in the United States of America
5240-(20)-9717

Foreword

Camping as an integral part of the program of Christian education continues to grow, and church camp leaders are constantly seeking better tools for a better job. A cycle of study was developed and presented in three books which have been used with Junior Highs during the past few years. Each book presented the philosophy of church camping in the program of Christian education as well as some of the aids for camping, so there was much duplication. These three books (*Living Together As Christians,* by Nelle Morton; *Stewards in God's World,* by John and Ruth Ensign; and *Camping and Christian Growth,* by Lynn and Campbell Loughmiller) were closely alike in their approach to developing the Christian community because their themes could not be clearly differentiated.

The content of these books has been brought together into one book with the idea that it will serve adequately in presenting the philosophy of church camping and in suggesting procedures for planning the program and training leaders. The three themes, along with suggestive program aids, are presented in one section under the chapter titles "Christian Community," "Christian Stewardship," and "Christian Growth." The leader should be familiar with all three and may use parts of each in a single camping experience, or he may use them in consecutive years, knowing what has gone before and what will follow.

The camper's *My Camp Book* will be available for each of the themes. These will be revised from the original camper books to conform to the methods and materials of this book for leaders.

Experience in camping has deepened the conviction of church camp leaders that young people and Christian leaders living in small, intimate groups twenty-four hours a day for a period of time offers unlimited opportunities to learn about God and His gifts to man, man and his relationship to and responsibility to God, and man in his relation to his fellow men. Here the Christian community may realistically be developed and experienced.

John and Ruth Ensign were chosen to write this book because of their recognized leadership in the field of church camping. Their leadership at Camp New Hope, near Chapel Hill, North Carolina, has been an inspiration to many campers as well as to church camp leaders. They are extending their influence in the developing of Camp Hanover, near Richmond, Virginia. Their camping is a dedication.

Robert P. Davis, Director
Camping and Conference Leadership
Presbyterian Church U. S.

Richmond, Virginia

Contents

Contents

Part I
PURPOSES AND PREPARATION

CHAPTER 1

Purposes

THE church-sponsored camp for boys and girls provides opportunities for Christian learning and guidance that cannot be achieved elsewhere in the church's program of Christian education. A camping experience capitalizes on the natural interests of Junior Highs in doing things together in the out-of-doors. It puts them in small groups in a rustic setting where through their simple outdoor living they can actually have an experience in a Christian community living close to the realities of God's world. In camping, Christian principles are not just discussed—they are also lived and evaluated. Here Christian stewardship is not merely studied—it becomes a way of life. Campers grow in purpose and ability through such cumulative spiritual experiences. As church leaders have experimented with and evaluated their camping experiences it has become increasingly clear that camping provides these unique learning opportunities, and so leaders have wisely left to the church school and the home those learning experiences that can be had better there. Thus camping does not try to duplicate the learning opportunities provided by the church school. Instead, by making full

7

use of its own possibilities, camping becomes an integral part of the total program of Christian education.

The church camp should provide an experience in Christian living which makes full use of the natural resources of the environment; helping campers to encounter God at work in the processes of creation in the world about them, to realize their dependence upon God for life and its necessities, and to grow in their understanding of God's will and purpose for His world. The relaxed pace of camping allows time for discovery, reflection, and wonder; for the reordering of personal values; and for the centering of one's life within the divine context. Worship attains a new measure of reality: it is a natural response. Through the daily activities of camping, the small group can have an experience in Christian living, motivated and guided by the Biblical revelation of God and of His will for man's life. Under the guidance of mature Christian counselors camp life can achieve a sense of wholeness, with the group moving at its own pace through a schedule of its own making, in which all experiences are brought into a Christian perspective. There is no artificial interruption of activities and no distinction made between experiences labeled "spiritual" and "secular." Life is whole and holy, it is re-creative, and it is joyous because it is good! Fellowship is real because the members of the small group, constantly living together, sharing responsibilities and insights, come to know one another with a depth of feeling seldom experienced elsewhere within the church.

Jesus spent a great part of His life in the out-of-doors. Much of His actual teaching took place in the open, on a hillside or by a lake, and He drew upon the things of the world about Him for many of His illustrations concerning God's will for man's life. He lived and worked intimately with a small group of disciples, concentrating much of His ministry upon them so that they could come to a personal realization of His mission. He also took time to go apart from men for quiet hours of prayer and meditation in close communion with God, His Father.

Much of our education comes through books others have written, or through the mass media of radio, movies, and television, and even much of our religion is based on what others have said. Until we have had personal experience our faith lacks conviction and vitality. Camping provides just such primary opportunities: to see and feel oneself a part of the good world God has created, to realize the dependability of God's laws controlling the universe, to sense the plan and purpose of all creation; to experience the depth of Christian fellowship within the small camp community of believers; and to come to an awareness of man's position as a steward of all God's blessings.

In order to achieve its unique possibilities most fully, church leaders must see the camp as a 24-hour-a-day opportunity to put into practice the Christian principles we so often only talk about in church. The camp setting provides campers with countless opportunities to deepen their understanding of God and His purposes, to see Christian love in practice and discover more satisfying ways of living in group situations, and to have the freeedom under loving guidance to grow as God intended them to grow. In the new environment of camp, campers are free to try out new patterns of behavior, to give their best in a group where every individual is a valued member no matter what his background may be, to emulate a Christian leader who is a constant companion, and to develop new skills and abilities. Camping can be one of the most meaningful of all the experiences in the total program of Christian education because it is a more unified experience, more intense and all-encompassing.

CHAPTER 2

Essentials for a Junior High Camp

IN planning for the most effective camping experience for Junior High boys and girls, there are some essentials which must be considered in order to achieve our purposes and meet our program needs.

Our Campers

A Junior High camp is planned for boys and girls of ages 12, 13, and 14 years, or those who are in grades 7, 8, and 9. The range of physical and social maturity is great in this age, and leaders must take this into consideration so that the campers will be in groups where they will not be overly self-conscious because of their stages of development. Special care should be given in forming groups, due to this physical and emotional range and their previous experiences.

The Camp Setting

Camping is simple outdoor living and the camp should be:
Simple and rustic, away from congested or frequently used areas, and a place of natural and unspoiled beauty.
A rough-and-ready environment lending itself to exploration, with plenty of natural resources to discover and use.
A place for informal living in group areas that have privacy and a sense of separateness. Adequate provisions should be made for health and safety in all areas of camp life.

Housing

Housing should allow each group of four to six campers and their counselor to live in one separate shelter. Double cabins and dormitory arrangements are sometimes unavoidable, but all effort should be made to seek separate shelters for each cabin group.

The Size of Camp Groups

The shelter group should consist of one counselor to live with each shelter group of four to six campers, not including the additional camp administrative personnel.

The small group is the co-ed camping group of one boys' shelter group with their counselor and one girls' shelter group with their counselor, who work together in planning and carrying out their own program, and developing their own small group campsite. A group of twelve Junior High campers (preferably eight to ten) is the maximum number two leaders can work with effectively in building group rapport and in meeting individual needs.

The total camp group should be limited, the ideal number being about 60 campers, and the maximum should be no more than 72 campers. When there is a demand for more, there should be two or more camps, with separate directors and staff for each.

Leadership and Training

Leadership should consist of mature Christian men and women who are willing to give their full time and attention to the campers in their group and who are prepared through training and actual experience to lead in church camping. Good leadership is the most important single factor controlling the success of a church camp.

Pre-camp training should be required of every counselor, and ideally of every staff member, and should consist of a minimum of three days, with at least two of them being consecutive days of actual camping at the campsite.

Length of Camp

Ten to fourteen days are recommended for the best cumulative effect. While camps of seven days are much more numerous than those of longer periods, campers in these shorter periods are just beginning to feel like a group accomplishing things together when it is time to leave. Every day beyond seven increases the effectiveness of the camp in achieving its purposes.

Preparation for Camp

A NY church camp which hopes to do a good job in Christian education through camping must realize the importance of adequate planning. It is no mere truism that the success or failure of a church camp depends on the quality of the preparations made for it. Planning begins months—even years—ahead, as the responsible committee carefully studies and agrees on purposes and procedures, selects and develops a campsite adequate for meeting their needs, chooses a trained director and staff who are in understanding agreement with the goals of the camp, and provides training for leaders so as to assure unity of purpose and familiarity with small group camping methods.

Church camping is only one part of the total Christian education program of the churches and as such should be planned in relationship to this over-all and ongoing program. By keeping the total program of Christian education in mind, the camp committee will seek to define its purposes and plan for those Christian learning experiences which are best achieved through camping, leaving to the church school and its programs the learning experiences which are better handled in a classroom situation.

Everyone connected with the camp needs to become familiar with the goals and procedures of church camping so that he can help interpret them to the larger church membership served by the camp. Only when there is understanding and a real sense of common purpose in Christian growth can there be a vital carry-over from the camp into the life of the local church. Many of our church members are honestly interested in their camp and what it seeks to do, and welcome an interpretation of the unique contributions it can make in the Christian growth of campers. Optimum results come when the sponsoring church, the camping committee, and the camp staff feel united in their common purpose.

The Staff

The staff—director, counselors, nurse, business manager, caretaker, cooks, and resource persons—will do their best when they feel they are in active partnership with the great ongoing program of the Church by carrying out its important mission for the churches back home. Such a sense of partnership gives the staff the security they need to be really creative as they seek new and better ways of working with Junior High campers.

The director should be a capable Christian leader, with a real grasp of the purposes, procedures, and potentialities of church camping and its relationship to the whole area of Christian education, and he must be a person who works effectively and democratically with both adults and young people. He should be a trained leader and dedicated to his task. Camp directing requires the giving of oneself at all times and the director must be able to meet the demands placed on him with Christian grace and understanding—and a sense of humor! It is also his responsibility to develop a working *esprit de corps* through staff training and to be in large measure the liaison between the camp and the churches.

The counselor should be a genuinely Christian person who lives and expresses his faith naturally in his daily relationships. He needs to understand the purposes and procedures of church camping and be able to lead his campers with enthusiasm in the exciting adventures of Christian growth that await them in camping. He must be a mature person, able to meet difficult situations with calm wisdom and understanding, and one who is primarily sensitive to the needs and interests of his campers.

A counselor's preparation begins the minute he accepts the challenge of counseling, with all its persuasive and specific demands.

1. Preparatory reading in the field of church camping. (See Bibliography.)
2. The training expected of a counselor; in pre-season sessions as well as in pre-camp training at the campsite.
3. The obligation of being in camp the full time required, with no expectations of leaving camp for any reason except in emergency cases.
4. Carrying out to full capacity his role of Christian friend and guide to his campers.

When counselors understand that they must fulfill certain specific obligations as a condition of their acceptance, they will plan to be on hand for the training sessions, and to be in camp the full time, even for the after-camp evaluation session. Ministers counseling in camp will make previous arrangements for pulpit supplies so that they can also fulfill their counseling obligations.

Pre-Camp Preparation

Some counselor training can take place at home or with other counselors in a non-camp situation. Individual reading of some of the basic church camp books will help a counselor in his understanding of goals and procedures. A guided reading program can provide valuable theoretical background on the philosophy of church camping and on ways of working with Junior Highs. Some camp leaders have found that a mimeographed handbook of their own program, given out months before camp, helps counselors to understand the general purposes and procedures of church camping in relation to their camp, as well as providing additional information on the history, traditions, and other pertinent information they need to know about the camp. Counselors can also practice some campcraft skills at home, such as firebuilding, cooking out, weather study, lashing, and nature study, with the help of books. (See Bibliography.) Counselors who live close to each other can gain immeasurably by practicing and studying together.

An early spring staff session in a church fairly accessible to most of the staff members is a valuable way of getting acquainted, stimulating thinking and preparation activities, discussing the goals and purposes of church camping, and planning for the coming camp.

Pre-Camp Training at the Campsite

There is no substitute for a *staff camping together* as part of its preparation, and every leader who expects to counsel in camp should be required to attend the pre-camp training session at the campsite even if he is an "old hand" at church camping. The teamwork necessary for a successful camp comes only through the staff living, working, and planning together for several days in the actual camp situation.

The pre-camp training period should consist of a minimum of three days (at least two of them consecutive days at the campsite) so that all the staff members can begin to merge their personalities and abilities into a working team. Ideally a week should be given to staff training to achieve optimum results. If a camp staff is going to guide boys and girls in co-operative democratic planning, then the staff must experience democratic planning in its own training program together. The staff needs the opportunity to evaluate objectives and, through the friendly give and take of discussion, to come to a basic agreement on its purposes and procedures. In co-operative planning each person brings to the discussion the best of his own thinking to be merged into a richer picture than any one could produce alone.

The best way for counselors to get to "know the ropes" and feel a measure of security as leaders is to camp together: planning menus, going through the process of getting food, and cooking it outdoors; constructing a simple shelter, learning the art of lashing and how to handle a pocketknife and axe; sleeping outdoors; using a compass, exploring; using discussion, worship, and fun spontaneously; capturing natural opportunities for Bible study and prayer; and acquiring other skills useful in camping, growing in their sense of being a team through camping together. To be most effective, pre-camp training needs to be relaxed. A hurried, frantic effort to cover a lot of ground in skills in a short time leaves counselors confused and less of a team than would a relaxed session covering only several basic procedures, including a cook-out.

Among the "Basics" for pre-camp training are the following:

1. Opportunity to become acquainted with the campsite and its natural resources.
2. Planning, preparing, and cooking out meals that are typical of ones Junior Highs may choose to prepare.
3. Opportunity to learn basic campcraft skills.
   —use of axe, pocketknife, bucksaw
   —compass
   —weather observation and prediction
   —sleep-outs
   —care of shelters
   —how to add additional protection with tarps in case of rain on a cook-out
   —fire building
   —tree and bird identification
   —lashing
   —nature games
   —craft work with native materials

   These are best learned by doing them as part of the staff's own camping together, so that the counselors will also realize the deeper meanings of the activity in terms of building fellowship, understanding the concept of stewardship, and growing in spiritual perception and action. Church camp leaders should constantly seek to understand the "why" of things as well as the "what" and "how." "It is more important to know the character of a thing as God created it than to know the name that man has given it."[1]
4. Sharing in worship, both spontaneous and planned. Worship should be as much a part of a training session as it should be of the campers' experience in camp. Counselors should be led to lift some of their shared experiences to the level of worship— praise, petition, and dedication—and to plan vespers as part of their group experience.

15

5. Singing together, gaining familiarity with good songs for use in camp, and experiencing the joyous rapport that singing helps to build.
6. Bible study, actually using the Bible in informal group discussions, decisions, and daily living together. The training session is a good time for a counselor to become familiar with the lists of suggested Scripture passages in this book so that he can work out an effective way of using them for reference help in working with his own campers later on.
7. Opportunity for asking all the questions on one's mind about leading in camp, to help increase the leaders' sense of security in knowing more of what is expected.
8. Opportunity for individual counselors to have time alone to formulate their personal objectives and plans for the camping experience.
9. Opportunity for the co-leaders of each small group to plan together—sharing their abilities, discussing their objectives, plans, and procedures, as a framework upon which they can build with their own small group. The "Counselor's Planning Section" (see Part IV) will prove especially helpful at this point in the training session. Counselors must remember that no program is complete without campers, and no planning in a democratic camp is final until the campers actually plan their program with the guidance of their co-leaders. Counselors can plan *for* program, but not plan *the* program. There's quite a difference!

Part II
PROGRAM GUIDANCE

CHAPTER 1

Small Group Procedures

Developing Program

In church camping, program consists of all the activities that are necessary for small group living in the outdoors, that are natural to the camp environment, and that are carried out in the spirit of Christian love. This is a program of living in which all activities flow into a continuous whole.

Program begins the minute the first camper arrives. For the first afternoon and evening, the counselor leads his group in orientation activities of his own planning, but the beginnings of group planning take place during this time in discussions of things the various individuals would like to do in camp, even to planning their first full day's activities together. Program grows out of the campers' needs and interests.

Camp living requires at least a minimum of necessary chores like keeping shelters and latrine areas clean, and assuming dining hall duties or cook-out responsibilities. These must be scheduled in the group's daily plans. The routine matter of accepting the responsibility

17

of observing mealtime hours, rest hour and bedtime, and the safety regulations for waterfront activities is essential to good camp living.

The counselor will find more specific help in guiding his group in program planning in the chapters in Part III which develop the three areas of emphasis for Junior High camping.

In planning their own program, campers are confronted with making real choices, bringing Christian principles and love to bear upon their decisions. The *way* a group solves its problems, chooses its activities in regard to minority viewpoints, adjusts to handicaps or disappointments, and puts into practice its Christianity, is program. The emergence of a particular plan of activities for one small group is the way its campers and counselors, with their unique combination of interests and needs, organize to camp together as Christians.

The Democratic Process

Small group camping enables each camper to make the maximum number of decisions affecting the life of the group. In the intimacy of a small group of ten or twelve campers and its two leaders, each person feels free to take his part in expressing himself and to assume his responsibility in group activities and decisions. The friendship and better understanding that develop within the small group encourage campers to speak more openly about their personal desires, and to feel more keenly their responsibility to each other for carrying out their part in activities to the best of their ability. Sometimes, even the majority in a small group will give in to the will of a steadfast minority in seeking the best solution to a group problem.

When program needs grow beyond the small group to a desire for activity with other groups, or a need for an all-camp decision, representatives may be chosen by each small group to meet with the camp director to work out plans or make a decision. Many camps feel it better to choose different representatives each time an all-camp decision is needed, in order to give as many campers as possible an opportunity to participate. Such all-camp decisions may involve the use of the Sunday offering, an all-camp play night of folk games or other activities, progressive suppers with different groups working together, and special Sunday activities.

Other camps find a planning session with the total camp group an effective way of helping the small groups plan co-operative activities with each other. Such a planning session should not take place until the small groups have had time to achieve a sense of groupness, and have worked out plans for their own group activities. In order to keep the planning session brief, only those activities involving the total camp

18

should be discussed and planned. Usually the camp director leads the session, writing suggestions and schedule plans on a blackboard for all to see. To facilitate discussion in such a large group, each small group elects a spokesman to present its ideas and decisions. When there is need during the planning session for the members of a small group to discuss a matter among themselves, before voting on final plans, each group can be given the same opportunity for a discussion, after which the spokesman for each small group will report his group's decision. Such a planning session actively involves every camper in the making of total camp decisions and gives all the campers a greater sense of actually determining their own program.

Flexibility in the Daily Schedule

In planning program a framework of "set times" for all-camp activities such as meals, rest hours, or all-camp vespers and campfires is set, leaving large blocks of time in which the small groups can schedule their own activities. Camp chores are also worked into this schedule—some, such as dining hall duties, at the specified time and others at whatever time the group wishes to work them into its daily schedule.

This flexibility is provided to give the groups the freedom to plan for longer activities. Sometimes a group will schedule an all-day exploration hike and will make plans with the dietitian for either taking a bag lunch or cooking out on the trip. Sometimes one small group will swap camp chores, such as dining hall duty, with another group or double up on duties one day so that they will be able to plan a whole day for activities away from the main camp area. Rising and bedtime are left somewhat flexible so that a group may feel free to retire early in order to go out quietly the next morning for a bird walk or to go fishing. Another group may be so engrossed in discussion around the embers of its campfire that, rather than abruptly cutting the discussion short for bedtime, the counselors taper it off or make plans to continue it the next day, and help their campers get to bed without disturbing others. However, counselors should keep in mind the required hours of sleep their campers need and should act accordingly.

In the "Counselor's Planning Section," a sample camp schedule for a small group is given. At first the scheduling of future activities should be considered tentative, dependent upon the weather, a change in group desires, or the adjustment to other all-camp activity plans.

Balance Between Small Group and Larger Camp Group Activities

During the first days in camp, counselors will seek to encourage the feeling of "groupness" and rapport among the members of the small

19

group so that a real Christian community spirit has a chance to develop. As the camp period goes on and a strong sense of groupness emerges, the campers will begin to desire activities involving other campers, enlarging their horizons to include others in their fellowship. This leads naturally into activities involving several small groups for progressive dinners, shared vesper programs, and various other activities. Later such all-camp activities as game nights or fun campfires may be planned. By allowing the small group to get going first, campers find security in a new situation within their own group before having to "sink or swim" in larger camp activities where they might feel lost on their own.

Refreshments

Camp nearly always means healthy appetites, and while dining hall food should always be hearty and wholesome, groups living outdoors will often desire refreshments. In a church camp there are better ways of meeting this need than through a camp store for soft drinks and candy.

Many camps plan refreshments as part of their program, even to including the cost of them in the over-all registration fee. Such a plan does away with the inequalities of spending money, provides more wholesome food for between-meal snacks, and gives the small group a budget within which to plan its own refreshments.

The dietitian can prepare "Refreshment Order" forms listing available items and their cost. Refreshments are ordered from the dining hall, usually at least two meals ahead of the time they are wanted. They may include such things as fruit, lemonade or punch, cookies, marshmallows, the ingredients for ice cream to be made in a hand freezer by the group, or pies, cookies, or cakes baked in the group's own oven at its campsite. Everyone in the small group is charged on a pro rata basis, with the counselors being responsible for keeping accounts within the budget.

CHAPTER 2

Opportunities for Worship

Spontaneous Worship

Living close to the things of the physical universe can bring us closer to the God who created them. Moments of worship can come unexpectedly in camp and a sensitive counselor will be alert to experiences in which campers seem to become conscious of God's presence: a feeling of joy and thanksgiving at the discovery of a refreshing spring on a hot, dusty hike; appreciation for a lovely green mossy spot deep in the woods; a sense of awe at the timelessness of God's creative purposes as revealed in fossils and rock strata; expressions of joy in friendship, of guidance for group problems, and of thankfulness for help in getting a difficult job done well; the sense of wonder at man's place in God's plan as campers encounter the magnitude of God's creation in the starry heavens at night, or view the vastness of the valleys from a mountain height. Sometimes a moment or two of silence eloquently echoes the thoughts of the campers and is worship. Sometimes a camper will speak spontaneously his deeper thoughts and lead the others in worship. On-the-spot, God-centered discussion can be worship. At other times the counselor will need to express his ideas, or recall an appropriate passage of Scripture that will give depth and meaning to the campers' awareness of God. And sometimes a familiar hymn sung softly is all that is needed to capture the experience of God for the group. As the group grows closer together in their camping, they come to appreciate and use more fully these spontaneous opportunities for worship.

Individual Meditation

Camp is an ideal place for Junior Highs to begin to experience the value of personal worship. Many mature Christians look back on their early church camp experiences with gratitude for the start they got there in the habit of daily prayer and meditation.

Morning watch is a time, either before breakfast or shortly after it (the choice probably dependent upon the desire of the small group), in which the members of a shelter group separate and each person finds

21

his own spot outdoors for meditation and Bible reading. For each of the three areas of emphasis there is a guide, *My Camp Book,* planned to be helpful in these times of personal worship. Most campers, especially new ones or younger ones, will need suggestions from their counselor about how to make the most effective use of these individual worship times. A counselor may also need to help some campers locate a particular passage of Scripture in their Bibles or help with hard-to-understand words before the campers go out to their worship spots. Very often the material in *My Camp Book* will start the campers thinking along lines that will heighten their perceptions and deepen their understanding of the experiences to follow during the day.

There is another aspect of individual meditation that needs to be encouraged: the writing down of personal thoughts, observations, prayers, dedication, and paraphrases of Scripture passages. Campers, through this experience, can grow tremendously in their ability to express themselves. Later when the small group wishes to do something like writing a litany together, the campers will be better equipped to share their ideas. *My Camp Book* has space in which the campers may write. Some campers may prefer to start keeping a spiritual diary of their own in which they will put their thoughts concerning God and their personal lives.

Evening devotions within the shelter group often consist of sharing personal feelings about the day's activities, and are closed by lifting the entire experience to the level of corporate thanksgiving in prayer. Many counselors feel that this sharing time within the cabin group can profitably begin with individual devotional reading in *My Camp Book,* along with the reading of the suggested Scripture passage.

Planned Worship

Each small group will want to plan some worship services of its own such as vespers or a special dedication service for a work project they have done. Sometimes the small group will plan the worship service together and at other times a special committee for the group may plan it. Campers can be encouraged to express and carry out their own ideas with counselors helping but not dominating, perhaps suggesting various possibilities for changes where they are really necessary so that a choice is still open to the campers.

There will also be opportunities for worship in the larger camp group.

1. An opening campfire which is essentially a worship experience to help set the spiritual tone of the camp. It is usually led by the camp director. (See "Special Program Helps.")

2. A shared vesper program in which several small groups, or the whole camp, join together. This may follow a progressive dinner at two or three campsites with each of the groups involved contributing to the service, or one of the groups may lead the whole service they have planned.
3. A hymn sing.
4. A sunrise service.
5. A campfire service of worship.
6. Sunday services. In some camps the service is traditionally a church service. In other camps each small group contributes in the leadership of the service: group-created litanies, prayers, meditations, choral reading, music, or the paraphrasing of Scripture. Such a service can be very meaningful to Junior Highs.
7. Dramatizations of Bible stories acted out at an evening campfire or perhaps on a Sunday afternoon on an open-air stage in a lovely part of camp. (See "Use of Creative Activities.")
8. A dedication service for the different service projects the various small groups have engaged in and completed. (See "Special Program Helps.")

Use of the Bible

The Bible is the basic resource for Christian living. In any program of Christian education which seeks to bring a person into a personal relationship with God, the Bible must be used in such a way that GOD may be made known through the revelation of His will and purpose for man's life and for our life now. God revealed Himself and His will through His dealings with the prophets and apostles, and supremely through Jesus, but this revelation is most compelling and meaningful when it is related to our own lives and the situations in which we find ourselves. To relate our lives to God and His will also binds us in deeper fellowship with those who responded to God in the Biblical account and brings us to a deeper awareness of our destiny as children of God. This is what is meant by encountering God through the Bible, by discovering Jesus and finding that He has a claim upon us!

To use the Bible thus is not merely to aim to learn facts about it or to use its passages in a proof-text approach, but rather is to relate its message to our present camp life in such a way that God can speak directly through His Word to the lives of the campers—to their problems, in their worship, and to their personal aspirations. The counselor will try to help his campers by asking: What does this say to you for our group life? What does this mean in your life? What is meant by this passage? The whole concept of Christian community, of Christian stewardship, and of Christian growth centers in the Biblical revelation of God's will for group life in the redeemed and redeeming community, of God's will for man's life as a steward of the resources of the earth and of his own life, and of God's seeking to win each person away from willful self-centeredness to eternal life in Him, the Source of all life.

To a great extent, how much and how well a group uses the Bible is dependent upon the counselor, his awareness of opportunities to make effective use of the Bible, his familiarity with and understanding of appropriate and helpful passages, and his ability to stimulate his campers in their searching for answers to the problems of life. A counselor will want to give advance thought to the "Helpful Scripture Passages" found in the chapters on "Christian Community," "Christian Stewardship," and "Christian Growth" in Part III of this book. It may also be helpful to jot down in the "Counselor's Planning Section," Part IV, some thought-provoking questions or other ideas which could be used in relation to specific passages of Scripture.

Use of Other Worship Resources

The counselor will find many suggestions for developing and using prayers, litanies, drama, poetry, and stories in the three chapters in Part III, "Christian Community," "Christian Stewardship," and "Christian Growth." Each of these chapters has a special section, "Resources in Prose and Poetry," which includes appropriate poems, brief illustrations, and stories.

24

Campcraft

1. Developing the Small Group Campsite

Each small group needs its own campsite, its own home in the woods. It is here the group will do most of its living: discussing, praying, and planning together; building, cooking out, and sleeping out; and enjoying pow-wows around a campfire. In some camps, each group is allowed to choose its own site and develop it according to its own desires with due regard for preserving the natural beauty of the area, privacy from other groups, distance from the main camp area, availability of water and firewood, and other necessary considerations. To choose such a site means exploration of available camp areas, discussions and evaluations, and finally a group decision.

In other camps, sites have been selected and partially developed, and each small group is assigned the use of one. A new group may be helped to feel a sense of stewardship toward its campsite which deepens its identification with it. Realizing that the campers before them have developed it thus far and left it in good condition for them to use increases the new group's desire to improve it for its own enjoyment and to leave the site even better for those who will follow.

In some camps, sleeping shelters for boys and girls will be a part of the total small group campsite so that almost all of the group's actual living will center right there. In camps where sleeping facilities are located in more centralized quarters, a small group may wish to construct a shelter at its own campsite to enable the boys and girls to take turns sleeping at the site, or to construct two simple lean-to shelters in separate areas near the campsite for boys and for girls.

2. Servicing the Small Group

It is imperative that some provision be made for servicing the small groups, enabling them to get materials and equipment for their activities when they need them. Usually one person is responsible for doing this, having stated times for being at the "Service Center" to give out tools and materials stored there and to check in equipment that is being returned. He needs to be a person who is thoroughly

25

familiar with all aspects of small group camping and who appreciates how much his job affects the over-all program of the camp. He will often be called upon to give suggestions and help on campcraft problems and he needs to be able to anticipate group needs such as when rain suddenly threatens a group's cook-out or sleep-out and extra tarps are needed.

Every small group will need some basic equipment on hand for its campsite. The following equipment is suggested:

Kitchen Area

1 per person plus two extra for guests Knife, fork, spoon, plate, cup, bowl.
3 Extra teaspoons
3 Serving spoons
1 Butter knife or 1 extra knife
1 or 2 medium and 1 large mixing bowl
1 Serving platter (very helpful)
2 Extra plates
2 Extra bowls
1 Saucepan
1 Stew pot with lid
1 Iron skillet #10
1 Dutch oven (large)
2 Pie pans
1 Sterilizer kettle
1 Sterilizer rack
1 Pair tongs
1 Dishpan
3 Water cans
1 Strainer or colander
1 Can opener
1 Butcher knife
1 Paring knife (use pocketknives too)
1 Sift spoon

1 Stir spoon
1 Cooking fork
1 Spatula or pancake turner
1 Measuring cup
1 Measuring spoon set
1 Plate scraper
Sponge cloth (dishcloth)
Scouring pads
Scouring powder
Soap
Salt and pepper
Paper napkins
Paper towels
2 Pot holders
1 Roll aluminum foil
1 Roll wax paper
#10 cans (about 8 with handles made from coat hangers)
Bushel basket
Half-bushel basket
2 large lard cans for making an oven
1 & 2-lb. coffee tins for food storage, or, glass jars with tops for food storage

Tools

Hand saw
Buck saw
Axe
2 Iron wedges for log splitting
Pliers and wire cutter
Short-handled shovel
Mattock-pick
Sharpening stones (for axe and pocketknives)

Other Equipment

First-aid kit
Snake-bite kit
2 to 4 Wash basins
Lantern
Matches in tin box
Binder twine
Toilet paper
Kitchen tarpaulin
4 Tarpaulins for shelters (16'x20')

26

All pots, baskets, tools, first-aid kit, and lanterns have group numbers painted on them for ease in identification. It is important when ordering food for cook-outs, refreshments, or drinks, that the cans or baskets with the group number on them be in the dining hall for the cooks to put the order in. The group number should also go on all refreshment and food orders.

Campcraft Construction—Developing a Small Campsite[1]

These are the construction projects that will be useful in developing a small group campsite:
1. Clearing a circle for cooking and eating.
2. Building a raised fireplace.
3. Making a pit lined with rocks for barbecuing and pit (imu) cookery.
4. Sawbuck for sawing up logs.
5. Chopping block.
6. Woodpile with cover.
7. Tables for food preparation and serving.
8. Rustic benches for sitting.
9. Reflector oven, or drum type oven out of lard can.
10. Shelves and storage racks.
11. Shelters.
12. Latrines.
13. Hand-washing arrangement.

Here are a few other construction and service projects suitable for small group camping:

1. Bridges—using lashed saplings over logs.
2. Trails.
3. Outdoor worship spots.
4. Signs and trail markers.

27

Here are a few stewardship facts to remember in construction in camp:

1. Cut only saplings that are needed and will be used.
2. Choose saplings that are crowded by others, stunted in growth, or for other reasons have little chance of making timber trees.
3. Make a clean cut with a saw as near to ground as possible—don't leave pointed stob to injure other people.
4. Select saplings from a wide area so as not to deplete any one area unduly.
5. Avoid overclearing undergrowth which is useful in holding soil and in giving a screen of privacy.
6. Run paths on contour of hills instead of straight up the grade so as to prevent erosion.
7. Keep paths to a minimum—avoid having paths all over the woods.
8. Mark trails, if necessary, with stones, or paper tied to trees. But never blaze a tree—this is not done today, as a blaze is a wound that hurts a tree as much as a cut on a man's leg hurts him.
9. Avoid contaminating small streams by dumping garbage and refuse into them. Dig a pit, or burn garbage.

Leaders will find a wealth of campcraft construction helps in the following books:

1. Catherine T. Hammett, *Your Own Book of Campcraft*
   Excellent on knot craft, lashing, and small projects. Not very helpful on shelter construction. A handy pocket reference that every counselor should have on hand at all times.
2. Bernard S. Mason, *The Junior Book of Camping and Woodcraft*
   A very useful general reference book. Has a satisfactory section on shelter construction of the traditional type. Not too good on wilderness shelter construction, using native resources.
3. Ellsworth Jaeger, *Wildwood Wisdom*
   By far the best reference when it comes to using native resources.

3. Cook-outs

Cooking outdoors is fun, and planning and carrying out a successful cook-out is an effective means of building group fellowship and rapport. The small group needs to consider the following in preparing a meal at the campsite:

(1) Their ability. Try simple menus and cooking methods first.
(2) Menu planning. Consider the seven food essentials for a balanced diet: milk, bread and cereals, green and yellow vegetables, fruits, meats and eggs, margarine, and potatoes or other starchy vegetables. Plan menu within budget limitations to provide hearty and tasty meal. Sometimes a group may plan an economy

meal like baked beans or chile con carne in order to have a more expensive pit-cooked ham dinner later on.

(3) Prepare food order for dietitian and turn it in at breakfast a day before the food is needed. The dietitian needs orders at least this far ahead so she can get the necessary food items which may not be on hand in the kitchen.

(4) Plan working committees: fire building, getting food and water to the campsite, preparing food and cooking, serving, cleaning up (including dishes, pans, leftovers, garbage disposal, and putting out the fire).

(5) The kind of fire or fires and wood necessary for cooking.

(6) The equipment necessary for preparing and serving the meal.

(7) The amount of time needed for preparing the meal, including the time required for getting the fire right for cooking. The time factor must also be considered in view of what follows the cook-out: if an all-camp vespers or other program follows, the group must be good stewards of their time so that they will not delay the other groups.

Ordering Guide

(Dietitian may add price per unit to aid small group in
calculating costs in relation to camp food budget)

Meat

Boneless (Steaks, liver, sausage, hamburger)	1 lb.	Serves 4 (1 lb. hamburger with oatmeal or crushed dry cereal can be stretched to serve 7)
Meat with small amount of bone (Round steak, pot roast, ham, rib roasts)	1 lb.	Serves 3
Stew meat	1 lb.	With vegetables can serve 8
Poultry		Allow 1 lb. per person 4 lbs. chicken creamed serves 10
Fish	1 lb.	Serves 2 or 3
Canned fish (tuna, salmon)	1 lb.	Serves 5 or 6

Vegetables   (Note: 1 No. 2 can usually serves 5)

Asparagus	20 stalks	Serves 3 or 4
Beans, green	1 lb.	Serves 4
unshelled limas	1 lb.	Serves 5
dried limas	1 lb.	Makes 2 1/3 cups, serves 2 or 3
navy and pinto	1 lb.	Makes 4 cups cooked, serves 4 or 5
Beets	1 lb.	Serves 3 or 4
Cabbage	1 lb.	Cooked serves 4, as slaw serves 5 or 6
Carrots	1 lb.	5 or 6 medium carrots, cooked serves 4

29

Corn	4 ears	Cut and cooked serves 2
Lettuce	1 head	Usually makes 4 or 5 wedge salads or serves 7 or 8 in tossed salad with other vegetables.
Onions	1 lb.	5 to 8 medium-size onions
Peas	1 lb.	When shelled and cooked serves 3
Peppers, green	1 lb.	7 peppers
Potatoes	1 lb.	3 medium, yields 2 1/3 cups diced, 2½ cups mashed and serves 3
Spinach	1 lb.	1½ cups, serves 3
Squash, summer	2 lbs.	2 cups cooked, serves 4
Tomatoes	1 lb.	3 to 5 medium tomatoes

Fruit

Apples	1 lb.	Approximately 3
Applesauce	2½ cups	Serves 5
Bananas	1 lb.	About 3, 2 cups sliced
Berries	1 qt.	Serves 4 to 5
Cherries, sour	2 lbs.	Sufficient for 9″ pie
canned	1 No. 2	Sufficient for 9″ pie
Peaches	1 lb.	3 to 5 peaches, 2½ lbs. approx. for 9″ pie
Pears	1 lb.	3 to 5 pears
Juice	1 No. 5 can	Serves 10 to 12

Cereal and Bread

| Dry cereal | Average box | Serves 8 to 10 |
| Cooked cereal | | Usually the given amount of cereal to 1 cup liquid will serve 2 |

Other Items

French dressing	½ pt.	Sufficient for 8 salads
Ice cream	1 qt.	Serves 4-6
Macaroni	1 lb.	Cooked serves 10
Popcorn	10 oz.	Serves 10
Rice	1 lb.	Serves 10
Sugar	1 lb.	2 cups

Methods of Outdoor Cooking

1. *Toasting on a stick* (hardly challenging enough for Junior Highs)

    Toasting frankfurters, buns, toast, marshmallows, cheese sandwiches.
2. *Stick broiling*—over hardwood coals. Largely individualized. Peel stick and heat it before putting on food. Taste bark. If bitter do not use stick. Find another.

    Pioneer drumsticks—use hamburger, mix with egg and crushed cornflakes, and seasoning. Squeeze in place around a stick about the size of a broomstick.

Kabobs—one-inch squares of beef ¼ inch thick, carrots, potatoes, and small onions alternately placed on a thin but firm green stick. Sticks trimmed to a square shape hold vegetables better. Oysters, ham, frankfurter pieces can be used instead of beef.

Steaks—fastened on twisted end of stick.

Bread twist—Use biscuit dough. Twist dough rather thinly around stick the same size as for Pioneer drumstick. Turn slowly over coals. Do not let it brown until dough has expanded to twice its size on the stick.

3. *One-pot meals*

Barbecued hamburger—real good served over baked potatoes! Use hamburger, tomatoes, onions, peppers, seasoning, and barbecue sauce to taste. Fry hamburger lightly and then add all ingredients and cook together in a #10 can.

Stews—Use leftover meats, stew beef, or hamburger. Add potatoes and other vegetables.

Slumgullion—hamburger, ¼th as much bacon, onions, tomatoes, ¼th as much American cheese, seasoning. Fry diced bacon and then add onions and hamburger. Cook until meat is browned. Add tomatoes and cook fifteen minutes. Add cheese cut in small cubes. Stir till melted.

Rice and salmon—an excellent, hearty one-dish meal on a hike where food has to be carried quite a distance. Cook rice, add canned salmon, sliced green pepper, chopped celery, can of peas, and cook until vegetables are tender. Season to taste.

Chili con carne, savory beans, and chowders are other good one pot meals.

4. *Baking*—in a reflector or drum oven.

Pies—Use packaged piecrust mix and native or canned berries or fruit.

Biscuits, cookies, and cake from prepared mixes.

5. *Cooking directly in the coals*—Be sure there are only coals; pull all flaming wood from fire.

Potatoes wrapped in mud or placed in a #10 can with sand between the potatoes.

Roast corn in the shucks—wet corn first.

Steaks (1-1½" thick) cooked right on coals—delicious for a special treat.

Aluminum foil cooking—double-fold all seams to prevent juices leaking.

Potatoes wrapped in foil.

31

Hamburger patty or steak with sliced potatoes, vegetables, seasonings, all wrapped
and sealed together in foil.

Tomatoes or peppers stuffed with pre-
cooked meat and vegetables, seasoned.
Wrapped in foil.

Fish fillet buttered and seasoned. Wrapped
in foil.

6. *Imu cooking*—cooking in pit lined with rocks, full of
coals. Place food wrapped in aluminum foil or grape
or sassafras leaves (or in Dutch oven) directly in coals,
then cover with more coals. Cover with a damp burlap and finally cover over with 6″ of earth to seal in
heat. Allow 1½ times the regular oven cooking time.

Baked beans in Dutch ovens.

Ham wrapped in grape or sassafras leaves or aluminum foil.

Chicken wrapped in wet leaves and foil.

Fish wrapped in foil.

7. *Spit cooking*

Chicken—Use barbecue sauce for basting.

Rouladen—Use beef ½″ thick. Salt and pepper
meat. Spread one side with mustard, then add
minced onion. Roll around pickle. Tie with
string. Spear the meat on a long green stick as
you would a hot dog. Sear quickly, then broil
slowly as desired.

8. *Reflector roasting*—roasting with heat from a reflector fire.

Planked fish on a board.

Ham or chicken suspended from wooden crane by
a heavy wet cord and constantly turned.

Menus and specific cooking directions may be found in Catherine
T. Hammett's *Your Own Book of Campcraft,* chapters 5 and 6. Your
own camp dietitian may wish to work out and have mimeographed for
small group use a food cost sheet including items, unit size and unit
cost, with ordering helps. She may also plan suggested recipe sheets for
outdoor cooking. These would be most helpful.

Fires[2]

There are many different kinds of fires for camping. Here are a
few basic facts to remember about fires:

1. Have a clearing around the fireplace. Build only on solid
earth, scraping aside all moss, leaves, roots, etc., for a radius
of several feet. Fire can go "underground" for many days
before breaking out many feet away. Be careful to build
your fire in a clearing away from trees that might be hurt
by it.

2. Build a fire only large enough for your needs. It is poor stewardship to waste extra wood on big fires. A large fire is also dangerous in the woods.
3. Have these things ready before building a fire:

   a. A small bag full of tinder. Dead twigs the size of a match, shavings of soft woods, or peelings of cedar or birch bark or splinters of fatty pine make excellent tinder. Any wood that will catch fire directly from a match will make tinder.
   b. Kindling. Larger dead twigs, and dry soft wood up to finger thickness in size.
   c. Fuel. General hard woods such as hickories, oaks, maples, and ash make the best fuel for steady, hot fires. However, first fuel wood after kindling can be a mixture of soft and hard woods so as to assure hardwood of catching from kindling. When fire is hot, use only firm hardwoods.
   d. Bucket of water or "Indian Fire Fighter" (standard water spray apparatus) for preventing the spread of fire. A fire rake and/or broom are also recommended.
4. Build gradually. Start with tinder, then kindling, and finally use small fuel. Add bigger pieces only when fire is going well. Leave plenty of space between sticks for air, but be sure each piece touches another for the fire to spread to it.
5. Never leave fire until completely extinguished. Good campers take extra precaution against the fire's getting out again. They always soak the ashes with water to make certain no fire is left. This is a part of good stewardship.

Types of Simple Fires for Cooking

1. The hunter's fireplace is called by many the best of all. The fire is built between two green logs, but two rows of large stones make a good substitute. The logs or stones act as supports for cooking pots, which are thus very close to the fire. Build a small fire and feed it only as needed. Coals are the best for cooking in this fireplace.
2. Trench fireplace. This is an adaptation of the hunter's fireplace. The fire is built in a trench 6 inches wide and sloping from 2 to 12 inches in depth. With a larger trench the fireplace can be lined with rocks and makes an excellent imu hole for pit cooking. When not used for imu cooking it can still be used for a regular trench fireplace and the rocks, when hot, help to make a steady source of heat. This way it is unsurpassed for barbecuing on a spit built above it.
3. Bucket fires. In places where fires cannot be built on the ground (city parks, mossy woods, pavilions, etc.), an old bucket with air holes cut in the bottom and sides makes an excellent stove. This can be fed with twigs and small chunks of wood, or charcoal.

33

It is an excellent wet weather standby as it can be used in a tent suspended from the ridgepole.

4. Tin-can fire or buddy burners. Small stoves can be made for individual cookery by utilizing #10 cans from the kitchen. Cut an opening in the bottom of one side for putting in the sticks for firing, and at the top of the other side cut several holes for a chimney. Leave one end of the can for the top and cooking surface. The opened end sits on the ground. Use small twigs for firing. Cook bacon, pancakes, eggs, etc., directly on the top.

5. The raised hearth fireplace. Where rocks are plentiful this is a great "back saver" and convenience. These fireplaces can be built with "dry wall" construction, or they can be made more permanent by using mud for mortar. They are exceedingly helpful in a permanent campsite where they can be used enough to make the effort necessary for their construction worth while. This construction makes a fine stewardship project using native materials. Another method of constructing these raised hearth fireplaces is to make a log cabin construction of green logs and fill in the middle with dirt. The fire is made on the dirt top.

6. Tin-can oven. This is made from empty lard or potato chips tins. Two cans are needed. One is supported on its side on green hardwood sticks or rocks to hold it about a foot above ground. The second can is cut open with tin snips along the side seam and then halfway around the bottom. This is then supported about six inches above the first tin to reflect the heat back on the other can oven. It doesn't take much fire to keep the oven hot. Sand placed in the bottom of the oven will help prevent burning. Anything baked in an oven at home can be baked in a tin can oven with a little more watching!

4. Shelter Construction

No other camp experience brings a deeper sense of being at home in the natural world and draws a group closer together in fellowship than sleeping outdoors in rustic shelters, and Junior Highs thrill to the experience. Even timid campers find the experience meaningful in the security of their group. Some camps may wish to build the more permanent rustic shelters like hogans, made from saplings bent covered-wagon fashion over either the ground or a plank flooring, and covered with a large canvas tarpaulin. Use a one-inch pipe to make holes in the ground and place the one-inch green saplings with ends

34

trimmed to one inch in these holes. On a wooden floor drill one-inch holes and run the saplings through the holes for stationary support. See illustration.

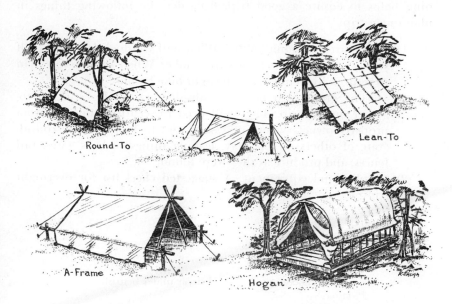

Small groups who do not have any sleeping facilities at their camp-sites may wish to construct simple shelters for their times of sleeping outdoors, such as the ones illustrated. The simplest shelter of all is made by stretching a rope between trees or other uprights and hanging a tarpaulin over it, staking its bottom edges to the ground in pup-tent fashion. Tab tents of the 10′x12′ size are an ideal size to use since they are easily handled by campers, need no poles as they are suspended from trees or other existing supports, and are of adequate size. Allow about 40 square feet per camper for living under canvas. (Consult your denominational headquarters if information is needed in buying tents or canvas.) Simple shelters to build are the hogan or covered wagon, the lean-to, the round-to, and the A-frame. Wood for shelters may be saplings (1″ to 2″ in diameter and cut with regard to good con-servation practices), bamboo poles, or 2″x2″ lumber like clothesline poles. Either tab tents or regular tarps can be used with these.

Shelter supports are lashed with strong binder twine. For lashing instructions refer to Catherine T. Hammett's *Your Own Book of Camp-craft,* chapter 8. Shelters will usually need to be ditched to prevent water from soaking the ground within them.

5. Hiking and Exploration Trips

Hikes and trips are more fun when you have what you need along with you and are not burdened with what you don't need. Wise planning helps to ensure a good trip. Consider the following things in planning a trip:

(1) Where are you going? Why? What will you look for? How will you get there? How long will it take? When should you plan to return? Remember, you have to hike home!

The group will need to consider reasons for sticking together on the trip. They will need to secure permission from property owners where necessary, and to be especially considerate of others on the way, leaving things such as gates, rail fences, and produce as they were found.

(2) Supplies and equipment. A suggested check-list for overnight trips:

Personal

> Bedroll or sleeping bag
> Jacket or sweater
> Raincoat or poncho
>> (also makes good ground cover under bedroll)
> Pajamas
> Toilet articles
> Extra socks
> Extra shoes or rubbers
> Hat
> 2 Bandana handkerchiefs
>> (for everything and anything)
> Pocket knife
> Compass
> Flashlight
> Bible and *My Camp Book*
> Canteen for water
> Pocket lens

Equipment

> Tab tents or tarps
> Axe (large and small)
> Shovel
> Binder twine
> Matches
> Soap
> Lantern
> Toilet tissue
> First aid kit and snakebite kit
> Insect repellent

36

Food and Cooking Equipment

See pages 28-34 for help on cook-outs. Check items against menu and type of cooking to be done. Don't forget salt and pepper and matches!

Who will carry what? Divide responsibilities.

(3) Take precautions for sunburn, chiggers, and mosquitoes, and watch out for poison ivy, poison sumac, and snakes. Here an ounce of prevention is really worth pounds of cure!

(4) Consider what to do if you get lost. It happens sometimes even to good campers, and all campers should know what to do if they get separated from their group. Counselors always need to watch the stragglers in their group so none get left behind.

Leaders need to prepare campers ahead of time concerning what to do if they should ever get lost

1. Shout in different directions—and listen!
2. Think, don't panic. From which direction did you just come? What landmarks did you pass? Observe the position of the sun in the daytime, or the North Star at night.
3. Climb a *nearby* hill or other lookout and try to find a familiar landmark. If your group is camping out, look for smoke to show where the campsite is.
4. Go downhill rather than uphill, looking for trails, brooks, or rivers. Chances are they will bring you to civilization sooner.
5. If you are lost and it's getting dark, prepare to the best of your campcraft ability to settle down for the night. Don't try to wander further unless you see a light *close* enough to reach safely.
6. Leave a trail so you will not wander in circles.
7. Remember, help is probably near. Besides, your group will begin looking for you as soon as they discover you are missing. Sometimes the best advice is to stay where you are until the group returns to find you. They will find you more easily when they retrace their steps if you haven't gone far and if you have left a trail.

(5) Take it easy on the way. Slow down to see things. Campers who want to achieve a sense of status by leading the group can be helped to find it in better ways—finding specimens and things to see, playing trail games, singing or telling stories. It is important to maintain a relaxed atmosphere so that campers will not be unduly tired. Junior Highs have an abundance of energy —to a point, and then they nearly collapse with fatigue.

(6) Be careful of your water supply. Carry water from camp or know safe sources of water on the way. Water can be made safe by boiling or with Halazone tablets if necessary.

37

(7) Evaluate your trip, discussing the things seen, enjoyed, and learned, and ways of improving the next trip. The mistakes made on a trip can be good learning experiences if a group is genuinely honest in its evaluation!

6. A Compass Trip

The most accurate means of telling directions is the compass. Junior Highs are fascinated with using a compass and enjoy planning and taking compass and map hikes, discovering in the process the dependability of another of God's laws for His universe. Inexpensive and easy-to-use compasses with directions for using them should be procured before camp opens.

7. Sleep-outs

A sleep-out should not be attempted too soon. Be sure your group is ready and prepares well. Comfort is a requisite for a good night's sleep and this is as true of sleeping outdoors as elsewhere. A little extra time spent making a place comfortable for sleeping is worth the effort. This means choosing a place that is free of humps, be they rocks—or pebbles!—, roots, or clumps of grass. Leaves, pine needles, cut grass, and moss placed under the ground cloth make the ground more comfortable and many campers, particularly those who sleep on their sides, like to dig a slight depression in the ground where their hips come. If the sleep-out takes place in camp at the small group campsite or near the cabins, by all means take your pillow along!

A ground cover to keep out dampness may be a poncho, waterproof canvas, an old plastic tablecloth, or a length of building paper.

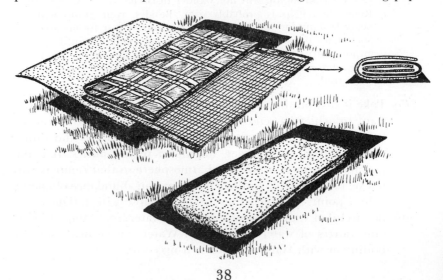

Some camps provide the latter. A bedroll is easily made with two or three blankets, folded together and pinned as shown in the illustration. When sleeping outdoors, it is necessary to have as much cover underneath as on top. A mosquito net is a necessity in many camps and can be stretched over lashed supports set in the ground over the bedroll.

Latrines should be dug conveniently close to the sleeping areas, being careful to locate them where they will not contaminate the water supply and where there is privacy. If bushes do not screen the area adequately a simple screen of old canvas, burlap bags, or brush can be lashed around it. Pile the dirt behind the trench that is dug and keep a shovel handy. Every time the latrine is used it should be covered with some dirt.

8. Use and Care of Tools

The pocketknife and axe are indispensable tools in camp but they are also potentially dangerous. Know how to use them and care for them.

The Pocketknife

1. Buy a good steel knife. Keep it clean, dry, and free of rust.
2. Keep it sharp. You are more apt to get cut trying to make a dull knife work than by a sharp knife that cuts as you want it to. Learn how to sharpen your knife.
3. Whittle away from you with due regard for the sweep of the blade when it leaves the wood you are cutting.
4. Don't walk with an open knife.
5. When finished with it (even momentarily) close it and put it in your pocket. You won't lose it, and you won't risk cutting yourself by absent-mindedly leaning or sitting on an open knife.
6. Pass an open knife only when necessary, and then with the cutting edge of the blade away from the hand and the handle toward the receiver.

The Axe

1. Keep it sharp. Use a chopping block of solid wood to cut your wood on whenever possible. It will save nicking the cutting edge of your axe. Never chop a piece of wood on the ground where rocks may nick it. Sharpening an axe blade is a tedious filing job.
2. Sheathe an axe when it is not in use. Keep it dry. During a clear day when the axe will be used a lot it can be kept in a chopping block. Never leave it in a block overnight as the block will swell with the night moisture and make it difficult to remove the axe.
3. When chopping be sure no branches, ropes, or other obstructions are in the way to catch and throw your axe. Aim your blow and keep your eyes on where you want to hit. Chop diagonally into wood, never straight in. Cut away from the butt of the tree or branch. Always place wood to be cut on opposite side of

39

chop block from your toes, and bend in knees enough so hands come below your knees at end of swing, thus ensuring that your foot or leg will not be chopped.

More specific help for using and caring for these tools is found in chapter 9 of Catherine T. Hammett's *Your Own Book of Campcraft*. All tools used by the small group, including craft equipment, should be used with a sense of stewardship; this means using them properly, and putting them away carefully when finished, so that they will be in good condition for the next campers who will use them.

9. Weather

Weather is an extremely important matter to a group living outdoors, and observing and forecasting become a vital part of a small group's program planning. With the use of some simple equipment, campers can learn to record and make daily forecasts. They can gain knowledge of instruments and their use, learn to recognize weather signs, recording what they find, and learn to use their observations in predictions. Observations should be made several times daily (perhaps before each meal), should be accurate, and should be recorded. Many camps have the small groups take turns in observing the weather and making daily forecasts to the whole group at mealtime in the dining hall.

Instruments that are needed are:
(1) A barometer (simple one made as in illustration).
(2) A thermometer—exposed to wind but fully shaded.
(3) Maximum and minimum thermometer.
(4) Wind vane—can be made (see illustration).
(5) Daily weather maps from U. S. Weather Bureau, Washington, D. C.

Small groups may wish to make a barometer and wind vane of their own to place with a thermometer in a good location near their own campsite. They can compare these readings with those of the instruments in the main camp weather station.

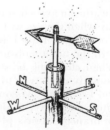

Glass tube in tight cork. Seal with wax so air enters through tube only.

Pop bottle ⅓ full of water. High or rising water level indicates fair weather.

String or rubber band to indicate fluctuations in water level.

CHAPTER 4

Use of Creative Activities

"Camping in the open is simple living, devoid of the pretensions and artificiality of much of modern life. It is informal living, and within the small group or the shelter group it is friendly and intimate in atmosphere. Such an atmosphere is one in which campers can feel free to express their real feelings and thoughts in their own way."[1]

Creative expression can be a *response* to an encounter with something—revelations of God in the beauty and magnitude of the created world; joy in fellowship; a beautiful or potentially beautiful rock, piece of wood, or other material, or even the arranging of plants and flowers to make them show more beautifully. Creative activities can also be a means of expressing *ideas* about things (stories or thoughts told in words, pictures, drama, or music) or *emotional reactions* to things (pictures and music that you feel, that convey a mood rather than express a tangible idea). Such activities deepen a camper's perceptions and help him to grow in his ability to understand and express himself.

1. *Writing*

Writing down thoughts and reactions helps to clarify ideas as the camper struggles to find the best words to say what he feels he wants to say. Writing should be an individual matter most of the time, but the group can have some very meaningful experiences as together they work out the ideas and words for litanies, prayers, poetry, or paraphrasing Scripture.

What to write? Stories, poems, observations, experiences, things that remind you of God, questions and wonderings about God and His world, prayers, dedications, paraphrasing Scripture in contemporary terms, or ideas for plays.

My Camp Book is designed to stimulate the writing down of ideas, and counselors can help the campers to make the best possible use of these opportunities.

Letters home are also a form of creative writing and are much more fun to write when a camper comes to think of them as a continued story of his experiences in camp.

2. *Drama and Role-Playing*

The aim here ought not to be "putting on a show," but coming to a deeper understanding of ideas and people through the physical means of expressing

41

these ideas in actions and words. The acting out of Bible narratives helps us to get inside another person's feelings and experiences and can even help us understand ourselves better.

A group can talk over the ideas involved, the ways of dramatizing them, and then play out the parts rather than writing them out to memorize. Such a drama changes somewhat with each playing of it. Sometimes a narrator can introduce or tell background parts of a story that are difficult to dramatize. Bible stories provide excellent drama possibilities and so do folk tales. Every camp should develop the historical stories and folk tales of its own locale and state, and especially those concerning its own camp area.

Other interesting possibilities with drama can be had by giving the play in pantomime and shadow behind a sheet-screen, or by making simple puppets out of native materials like cornhusks or pine needles, rushes or tall grass, bound in such a way as to make figures to be attached to sticks, by which they are moved. A genuine sharing of the actual feelings and experiences of a group through a dramatization, shadow play, or simple puppet show can actively involve as participants many otherwise timid boys and girls, and will be more worth while than the traditional "stunt nights" of many camps.

3. Painting and Sketching

This takes materials, and while you can sketch with just a pencil and paper, campers often find themselves frustrated trying to express their feelings with such limited means in the face of all the color in the world about them. Colored chalks and crayons are relatively inexpensive, and watercolor sets with brushes can be bought for less than a dollar. A camp could well invest in 10 or more such sets along with some good quality sketching paper. These could be kept in the "Service Center" where other extra equipment is kept, and be borrowed for use when a group is ready for such an experience. Some camps may prefer to provide enough materials for each small group to have its own always ready for use.

4. Nature Crafts

In all nature crafts and crafts using native materials care should be exercised to practice good conservation. When campers find what they need they should be sure that taking it will not appreciably deplete the supply, will not hurt the plant, and will not be a cause of future erosion. What to take, when to take it, how much to take, and how to take it, become real problems in conservation.

(1) Making displays for collections—rocks, leaves, feathers, different colors of soil placed in layers in a bottle, bird nests, shells, etc. There are many and various ways of mounting and displaying collections. Include identification. Share with other groups.

(2) Bird feeding stations made to hang on trees. Feed with seeds and scraps of food. Such stations may also attract squirrels.

(3) Bird baths, hollowed out of fallen trees or stumps. These can be lined with aluminum foil to keep the water from seeping away.

(4) Making plaster casts of animal and bird tracks. Put clipped cardboard frame around track. Mix and pour plaster. Allow to harden before lifting.

(5) Terrariums made in glass jars. Put in gravel first, over a few pieces of charcoal, add woods dirt and moss to cover gravel, and add tiny woods plants.

Water and cover with either screw top or piece of glass. Remove cover about an hour each day, water sparingly, and keep in a light but shaded place.

(6) Hanging flower baskets made of lashed sticks and twigs, lined with moss, the growing part showing through the sticks. Add earth, woods plants, and vines. Hang with wire or string.

(7) Aquarium, using glass jar (large empty mayonnaise or mustard jars from camp kitchen are fine for this). Put sand in bottom, add a few plants from stream or lake, and water from there too, being careful not to disturb plants. Add marine life that is found. If turtles and frogs are added, give them rocks above water on which to sit.

(8) Mount a small magnifying lens in a carved piece of wood to make a useful piece of study equipment.

5. Craft Work with Native Materials [2]

(1) Clay

Clay can often be found along stream banks, railroad or road cuts, excavations, or just under the surface grass in marshy places. To test whether the clay your group finds will be usable, spread a little of it out on a board to dry a bit. Then roll it into a piece about the size and shape of a pencil and coil it around the finger. If it does not crack it will be fairly workable. If it cracks, plan to add about 7% to 10% of bentonite or ball clay (available from local art stores or clay companies). . . .

Remove the large impurities of leaves, roots, and rocks when the clay is dug. Then spread the clay out on a board in the sun to dry. When it is dry chop it until it is fairly well broken up. Then fill a non-rusting container for the clay half full of warm water. Add the crushed clay until it forms a mound on top of the water. Don't stir. Let it stand overnight.

The next day sieve the clay through a fairly fine screen to remove more impurities. Let it stand again until the clay settles to the bottom and excess water can be poured off the top. Then spread the wet clay out on a board or on a large plaster bat to dry out more water until the clay is stiff enough to work without sticking to the fingers.

All clay needs to be well kneaded before working it. The freer it is of air bubbles the better it is. Campers will enjoy rolling and pounding it before making their figurines, bowls, or other projects.

Projects should be well dried in the air before any attempt is made to fire them. Let them stand in an open, dry place, where the air can circulate freely around them. . . .

A simple method of firing in camp is to put the clay pieces in a large lard can oven propped up on stones with a hot fire burning beneath it. Build up the fire gradually, keep it going all day, and then let it die down slowly. Clay pieces need to change temperatures slowly so that they will not crack. Let objects cool in the oven overnight. . . .

(2) Wood Projects

Dried cedar can be found in abundance on many campsites and makes excellent wood for craft uses. Other camps will find many other woods—rhododendron, laurel, walnut, apple, pear, cherry, birch—equally usable. The usual collection of simple tools—saws, chisels, hammers, drills, straight edges, and vises—plus a few finishing materials like sandpaper, steel wool, shellac,

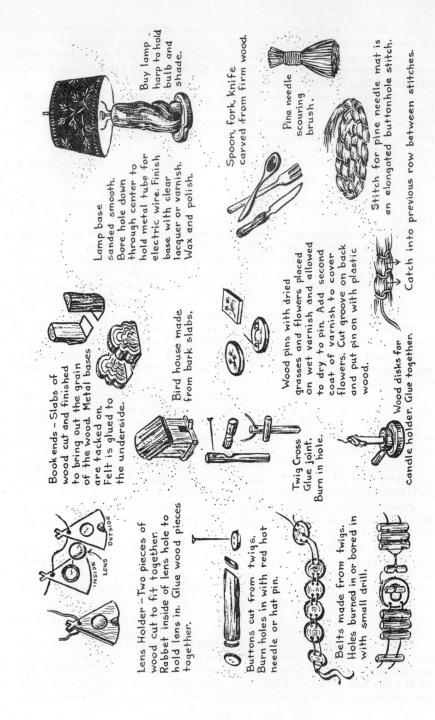

Buy lamp harp to hold bulb and shade.

Lamp base sanded smooth. Bore hole down through center to hold metal tube for electric wire. Finish base with clear lacquer or varnish. Wax and polish.

Spoon, fork, knife carved from firm wood.

Pine needle scouring brush.

Stitch for pine needle mat is an elongated buttonhole stitch.

Catch into previous row between stitches.

Bookends - Slabs of wood cut and finished to bring out the grain of the wood. Metal bases are tacked on. Felt is glued to the underside.

Bird house made from bark slabs.

Wood pins with dried grasses and flowers placed on wet varnish and allowed to dry to pin. Add second coat of varnish to cover flowers. Cut groove on back and put pin on with plastic wood.

Wood disks for candle holder. Glue together.

Twig Cross Glue joint. Burn in hole.

Lens Holder - Two pieces of wood cut to fit together. Rabbet inside of lens hole to hold lens in. Glue wood pieces together.

INSIDE   LENS   OUTSIDE

Buttons cut from twigs. Burn holes in with red hot needle or hat pin.

Belts made from twigs. Holes burned in or bored in with small drill.

varnish, clear lacquer, and wax, will prove adequate for making simple and beautiful projects of wood. . . .

Lovely pins can be made from small pieces of wood and pretty pieces of dried and pressed flowers and grasses. The wood background is varnished (shellac and lacquer dry too fast) and then the dried flowers and grasses are arranged in a pretty design on top. Allow them to dry into the varnish; they will stick to it. When dry, varnish over the whole pin—flowers and all.

(3) Weaving

Weaving can be done with the natural fibers of broad-leaved grasses, rushes, and cornshucks, the rounder fibers of honeysuckle and willow, the peeled tree bark from fallen trees such as birch, and from the splint fibers pounded from sassafras, white oak, ash, or scaly-bark hickory. All of these can be woven into mats, baskets, trays, or purses.

The grasses and rushes need to be dried evenly in the sun and then slightly dampened while being worked. Honeysuckle and willow shoots can either be dried and peeled of their bark, or boiled in soda water to loosen the skins. Soak these reeds in water when working with them to make them more pliable.

The splint fibers from sassafras, etc., are obtained by pounding a freshly cut log, causing the layers of wood to separate into strips for basket or mat weaving. These strips must be pulled apart after the pounding has loosened the layers.

(4) Pine Needle Projects

Long pine needles can be woven into mats (small for hot dishes, large for door mats) by taking a bunch of needles the size of a finger, tying one end securely with string, and then fastening the needles together into a mat using an elongated buttonhole stitch. More needles are added in a staggered fashion until the mat is the size desired.

Simple but very effective scouring brushes can be made from pine needles, whipped tightly with string into a handle at one end, and then cut off straight across about $1\frac{1}{2}$ inches to 2 inches below the whipping.

(5) Other Nature Craft Possibilities

Table decorations for the dining hall can be made from mosses, nuts, dried pods, pretty stones, and small plants arranged in shallow containers or on small slabs of wood cut at an angle from a branch of wood. . . .

Dyeing with natural dyes is an interesting adventure where cloth for dyeing is available. Sacks or unbleached muslin make good cloth. Berries, bark, tree lichens, onion skins, grasses, all produce their particular colors when boiled in water to a concentrated solution. . . .

Drawings can be made with various colored small stones by drawing with them on fine sandpaper.

Simple musical instruments can be made from willow or bamboo reeds, or cornstalks. Holes can be bored in the bamboo and willow with small metal bits, and can be burned into the cornstalks with a hot wire.

Gourds can be made into rattles by opening one end and dropping in a few pebbles. Seal with plastic wood. Drums can be made by cutting off one side of a fairly large gourd. Empty out seeds and cover opened end with tightly stretched oiled brown paper.

45

6. *Music and Choral Reading*

Campers may enjoy creating their own songs. This can be done by beating out the rhythm of a favorite poem or Psalm, and then making a tune to go with the rhythm. The group can try out quite a few "versions" of their song in order to choose the one they like best. The counselor or a musical camper can write down the tune so it won't be lost. Some campers may wish to create music for Psalms, poetry, or original verse themselves. Later at a piano the key and time may be decided on and perhaps a few changes made in the tune itself to improve it.

Scripture passages or poems may be arranged for choral reading with variations of high voices, low voices, solo parts, and choruses. Again the group will want to try several versions before choosing the one that seems best to them.

CHAPTER 5

Special Program Helps

1. First Afternoon and Evening in Camp (Including Opening Campfire)

First impressions are usually very strong and last a long time; it is important that arriving campers and their parents find a friendly welcome and prompt help to get the Junior Highs settled in their cabins. Registration should be brief, mainly check-in and cabin assignment. Fees should be handled in advance along with an understanding of grouping policies. Any materials for the campers should be given to them at their shelters.

Since counselors are already settled in their cabins they can be on hand to greet their first campers as they arrive and go with them and their parents to the shelter. Most parents like to see where their children will be, and an alert counselor can learn much by observing the parent-child relationship. At the shelter a camper can choose his own bunk and begin to get his belongings put away. While he is doing this, the counselor can talk briefly with the parent, getting acquainted, learning something about the camper, and, by his manner, establishing confidence. While helping a camper make up his bunk the counselor can engage in friendly conversation, helping to make the camper begin to feel at home. Simple refreshments like lemonade and peanut butter crackers on hand in the shelter are good, and early arrivals can even help to spread peanut butter on crackers for those to come.

It also helps to have other things for campers to do while they wait for the rest of their shelter mates to arrive. Whittling simple name tags out of wood is a good idea; it starts the campers right out learning to use a pocketknife, and the name tag helps others learn his name faster. Names can be printed on the small wood tag, or carved in. A $1/8$th-inch hole is drilled for the neck string of binder twine or natural cordage. The whole tag is waxed when finished.

When all the campers in the shelter group have arrived, the counselor can take them on a tour of at least the part of camp they will need to know first. A mimeographed map of the camp also helps them to get oriented, and if it is an accurate map it can be used later for compass hikes. If a counselor has a number of old campers in his

47

group, shooting an azimuth on the dining hall, for instance, puts a "new wrinkle" in orientation for them and whets an interest in use of the compass. A short swim is refreshing and can sometimes be worked in. Exclude a swim if it will rush a group too much: it is more important that camp get off to a relaxed and easy start, and there will be plenty of time for swimming in the days to come.

At supper the newly acquainted shelter group should sit together so they will feel free to ask questions and get used to dining hall procedures. Some singing can be done after the tables are cleared. A short period should be allowed after supper for personal chores and getting flashlights. Then the two shelter groups, one of boys and one of girls, that make up a small group will meet together for a get-acquainted time. Some games that help them to learn names and simple nature games can be played.

After the games when the campers are ready to rest a bit and the "ice" is broken, one of the counselors can lead into an informal discussion about camp. Questions like, Where are you from? and Why did you come to camp? are good starting ones, followed by, What would you like to do in camp? to help anticipate some of the camping activities that are possible for them. The group may also plan some of their activities for the next day. In some camps, the whole first night is spent in small group activities around their campfire, in the belief that adjustment takes place faster by giving campers more time to find security in their small group first.

Other camps like to have an all-camp opening campfire as soon as it begins to get really dark the first night. By having the small group sit as a unit, their sense of groupness is preserved while they feel themselves a part of the larger camp group. Usually campers will maintain silence and not use their flashlights during the campfire ceremony. It may be suggested to them to pray silently during the first quiet moments in the circle, asking God to help them have one of the best experiences of their life while in camp.

The camp director may use some of the following ideas for helping the campers to find real meaning in such a service around a campfire, making it really a religious experience:

> In the darkness of this circle we cannot see one another, and we are practically strangers. When we light this fire, even the small light of the match (or the first flame of the flint and steel fire) gives us some idea of those around us. As the fire grows we can see each other more and more clearly, until we can even make out the faces of those across the circle from us.
>
> The lighting of this fire is a symbol of what Christ can mean to us in this camp. We have come to camp as strangers to one an-

other. Many of our lives are in darkness, just as we were in darkness before lighting this fire. During this week of camping we have the opportunity of learning what Christ meant when He said, "I am the light of the world: he that followeth me shall not walk in darkness, but shall have the light of life." If Christ does come into the center of our living here, He will bring new light and love into all our friendships and our activities. If we do not bring Him to the center of our lives, we will be in darkness. So, just as we have lit this fire to start our camping together, let us pray that we can learn to live in the light of His life and teaching in the days ahead.[1]

A simple prayer and a few appropriate hymns—"Fairest Lord Jesus," "This Is My Father's World," "Lord, I Want to Be a Christian"— may follow. The director may wish to speak briefly about the larger company of campers of which these campers are a part; those who have preceded them in the use and enjoyment of this camp, who have left a part of themselves in the improvements they made as Christian stewards of God in the Christian community that is camp. He may wish to challenge them to grow "in wisdom and in stature, and in favor with God and man." A brief prayer and another hymn could follow before the groups leave the circle to go back to their shelters.

Bedtime the first night should be a quieting time: a few minutes to talk over the day; to give out *My Camp Book* and talk about it; to plan for quiet awakening activities the next morning that will not disturb others who are still sleeping, like reading in *My Camp Book;* to anticipate some of the night noises that may worry the campers, such as squirrels on the roof or owls in the woods; and to allow time for devotional reading and prayers before "lights out."

2. Rainy Day Activities

For the most part, camping activities are carried on as usual even if it is raining. Additional tarps and scrap canvas can be stretched to provide more protection at the campsite so that a group can continue to cook or build there. Sometimes, if it is storming too hard, a group could do as one group did, and cook their food over fires made in old buckets with holes punched in the bottom of them and suspended by wire from the ridgepoles of their shelter. Working together to overcome difficulties binds a group more closely and they have a lot of fun in the process. Campers enjoy being ingenious.

Rainy days are ideal times to work on craft projects from natural materials. These materials may have been gathered earlier or they could be gathered on a rain hike—wood for whittling and carving, vines, reeds, and grasses for weaving, and other items that can be used.

There are unique opportunities afforded by rainy days. Hikes in the rain can be a lot of fun provided campers are dressed properly and get back to their shelters to change clothes before they get too wet or chilled. In the rain, campers can see what water erosion can do when it is not controlled and they may be moved to undertake a service project to help control erosion, like building check dams or terraces, or transplanting seedlings and sod. Sometimes storms wash up driftwood and other interesting things along the shore. Scavenger hunts for things hard to find in the rain are fun—a dry leaf, a butterfly, a feather, etc. Or test a group's campcraft skill by building a fire in the rain, finding dry wood without raiding the woodpile. If the weather is warm and it is not during an electrical storm, take a swim or build a dam in a brook. Try having a boat race floating leaf or bark boats—it's silly but fun!

Other groups have used rainy days for telling stories, learning new songs, and taking more time in discussion and Bible study. Rainy days provide time for delving into resource books for ideas and information, for sketching and writing, and for working out dramas.

3. Sunday in Camp

Sunday is a different day even in camp, and activities should be in keeping with the best Christian ideas of worship and rest. It should be a re-creative day, a time to slacken the pace but not to the point of boredom. Through thoughtful planning, the day can be enjoyable and uplifting.

"Camp must not break down the feeling for corporate worship which the home church seeks to foster. Many church camps have their own traditional forms of observing Sunday morning worship."[2] The order and type of service and the place in which it is held will vary according to the desires of those planning the camp. Some camps also have a Sunday school time for Bible study and discussion growing out of each small group's needs.

There are some other special program ideas that can be used to make Sunday a different day.

1. One camp, plagued by the problem of Sunday afternoon visitors in spite of requests to the contrary, takes an all-afternoon, all-camp hike to a lovely place away from camp. A picnic supper is served there and vespers are also held there before coming back to camp for a watermelon or ice cream treat.
2. Bible charades may be planned in the small groups in the afternoon at their campsites and then after supper the whole camp may enjoy them together. Campers like this and really work out good ones.
3. Antiphonal or echo singing may be done from boats to land, across a lake, or from hill to hill.
4. Time may be allowed for visiting different campsites, seeing

what others have done, and getting acquainted with campers in other groups.

5. A special vesper service may be planned for the whole camp.
6. An extra long rest hour is always in order on Sunday afternoon.

4. Service Projects

A service project is an activity which seeks to make visible the campers' love and concern for God's world and the blessings He has given them, and to express their gratefulness through sharing and doing things for others. This motivation for activity cannot be forced; as the group grows in its feeling of being a little Christian community with a sense of their responsibility as faithful stewards of God's gifts, a desire to serve will naturally take place. What would be simply good conservation of resources to the average person, becomes an activity of dedicated Christian stewardship to the campers involved.

The idea of a small group's engaging in a service project activity may spring naturally from an experience in which they sense the need for "doing something about it." Sometimes it will be the counselor who first casually suggests the idea, knowing how much campers can grow through sharing in such a project. A group seeing the effects of erosion on a hillside may decide to construct some check dams or terraces, or to plant seedlings in an effort to keep more soil from washing away. Another group having to cross a rickety footbridge many times a day may decide to rebuild the bridge so it will be easier to cross even though their work will primarily benefit the campers who follow them.

Some service projects which have grown out of the experiences of other small groups include: the repairing of woods trails to check erosion, gathering and storing wood for firewood and craft projects for the use of future camp groups, building rock retaining walls, staking tree seedlings near cabins to prevent their being stepped on, constructing firebreaks, caring for an injured tree, constructing an outdoor vesper spot, gathering various native materials for future campers to have on hand for craft work, and generally improving the camp for the future.

There are other projects of helpfulness which may grow out of the campers' experiences. One group who had a foreign student as a counselor was so moved by her stories that they made a contribution to a mission project in her country and persuaded the rest of the campers to give the Sunday morning offering to this project. This, too, is service, although it is probably not as complete a form of service to Junior Highs, to whom money is given, as is a project involving their own toil and energy.

51

A service project should culminate in a simple dedication service, either shared within the small group or—for a project of particular benefit to the whole camp—shared with everyone.

5. Campfires

(1) *Small Group Pow-wows*

Group living of this sort enables each member to participate in the pow-wow, or evaluation, around the evening campfire. It is here, at the close of the day, that common experiences can be discussed; where one's mistakes and successes can be recognized; where one separates the good from the bad, the true from the false, the right from the wrong. It is here that the best insights and attitudes are developed. This is where the experiences of the day are evaluated more objectively and are seen in relation to the broader aspects of living. Man is apt to feel more keenly at these times his dependence upon the world about him, and to sense with greater than usual insight his relationship to God as Creator. This sometimes becomes worship—worship at its best.[3]

A perceptive leader will sense when a group is ready for serious discussion and sharing at the deeper level and will seek to create the climate for real participation and "letting down of defenses" by his questions and his objective sharing of his own feelings. Sometimes a group does not seem ready to respond in discussion; at such times the singing of folk songs and of hymns may prove a better way of strengthening fellowship, and sometimes the "fellowship of silence" around the embers of the fire may deepen the bonds of friendship more than anything else.

(2) *Fun Campfires*

Campfires for the sheer fun of it can be had either in the small group or in larger camp groups. The latter should be more definitely planned to avoid any elements of confusion in such a large group. Fun campfires are usually made up of storytelling, games, and singing.

(3) *Storytelling*

Folk tales, Indian tales, pioneer stories, and tall tales make good telling around a campfire.

—Richard Chase's *Grandfather Tales, The Jack Tales,* and his new 50¢ Signet Key Book, *American Folk Tales and Songs,* all have good stories in them. However, counselors should read through them first; some of the stories need minor changes in wording and a few are better not used with Junior Highs.

—Theodore Whitson Ressler's new *Treasury of American Indian Tales* (Association Press, 1957) is a good collection of Indian stories for young people.

—The Paul Bunyan tales, John Henry stories, and other folk
tales of a particular locale are also good to tell.

—Progressive tales, in which each person adds a bit to the story,
and "yarn swapping" give everyone a chance to participate.

(4) *Singing*

There are many excellent collections of songs for use with young
people put out in pocket-sized editions by the Cooperative Recreation
Association, Delaware, Ohio. *Sing It Again, In Harmony,* and *Songs of
Many Nations* are among these. Your denomination may also have one
of its own from this source. These are inexpensive songbooks so a camp
can easily invest in enough for all the campers to use.

(5) *Games*

Charades are lots of fun acted out at a campfire. Guessing games,
riddles, relays, and rhythm games are also good. (See "Basic Camping
Resources." Allan A. Macfarlan's *Campfire and Council Ring Programs* may provide additional help.)

6. Ways of Closing Camp

The last day is a time for bringing into focus the total camp experience; relaxed time for the campers to consider the deeper meanings of all their camp activities, to see the wholeness of their living
experience in a little community that sought to be Christian, and to
seek for ways of continuing and extending the experience into the
home situation. Some leaders call this "evaluation"; to the campers it
means finding answers to: What has camp meant to me?, What did we
learn through our activities?, In what ways did we experience real
Christian community?, and How have I grown in my understanding
of what living as a Christian means, and of God's will for my life?
Some of this evaluation will take place through discussion in the small
group, and some time should also be provided for purely personal
evaluation, allowing campers time to think and write by themselves.
Some campers like to write themselves a letter with some of their ideas
and personal aspirations in it, giving them sealed and addressed to
their counselors to mail to them at Christmas.

Many groups whose campsites will be used by campers following
them like to take time during the last day to prepare something special
for those who will follow. One group left a "Last Will and Testament
to the Campers Who Follow Us," willing to them some of the most
meaningful of their own group experiences, along with a full woodpile,
a collection of native materials for crafts, and a clean campsite—not
to mention all the chiggers they hoped they were leaving! Through

53

such activities campers turn their attention happily to the joys they hope others will have rather than thinking only of the end of their own good time together. In so doing, they are taking their first steps in extending their experience beyond their own camp days.

Some groups like to take time the last day to do again some of their favorite things—visiting a lookout spot whose view they cherish, checking on a special bird's nest, or quietly sitting together in the vesper dell for a few minutes.

The closing night service will have far more meaning for the campers if no effort is made to capitalize on the emotionalism of Junior Highs. This is the time when they will want to share their ideas in summarizing their camp experiences, seeing the ways in which they have grown personally, socially, and spiritually during the time they have been together. This is a way of strengthening their personal commitment to the way of life as revealed by Jesus: it can be a means of a personal encounter with God, and no attempt should be made in camp to make it a public commitment. That is better done in the home church fellowship. The closing service should not be long and "should serve as a sort of benediction to their entire camp experience."[4]

For the closing campfire service in one camp, each small group came prepared to share something from their evaluation period—litanies, poems, prayers, stories, some meaningful experience. Several hymns which had come to have special meaning to the campers were sung.

> Finally the director led the group in a period of directed meditation in which each camper had the opportunity to make personal resolutions and commitments to God. Silently the group watched the embers of the fire die down, and then, without talking, they moved quietly back to their shelters.
> Many camps have found the campers most appreciative of continued silence until the following morning, feeling that this forms an effective climax to the camping experience. However, it should never be imposed on campers by their leaders, but used only if the campers really want it.[5]

Other camps prefer to have their closing all-camp campfire early enough to allow the small groups sufficient time for their own last "pow-wow" together.

The following morning before the campers leave, many camps have a closing service of worship with the campers and their parents. Usually the service is quite brief, sharing with the parents some of the highlights of the camp experience, and seeking to bring before parents and campers the place of the camp experience in the larger framework of the fellowship of the church.

CHAPTER 6

Basic Camping Resources

1. Scripture Passages Related to the Outdoors

Genesis 12:1-9 —Abraham left his home at the call of God to
13:14-18 become a nomad living in tents. God's prom-
15:5-6 ises to Abraham were given in the outdoors.
Genesis 28:10-17—Jacob was sleeping on the ground outdoors
when God spoke to him assuring him of His
presence.
Exodus 3:1-12—Moses was in the wilderness keeping sheep when
God spoke to him out of the burning bush.
Exodus 19:16—20:17—God reveals to Moses His commandments
for His people living together in their
camp community.
Psalms 8, 23, 91, 104, 121—David came to know and trust God
during his long days and nights out in
the wilderness tending his sheep.
I Kings 19:1-18—God spoke to a disillusioned Elijah in the still
small voice in the wilderness.
Amos 1:1 and 7:14-15—God revealed His will for Israel to Amos
during the long days and nights he spent
as a shepherd of Tekoa.

Jesus spent much of His life in the out-of-doors:

Matthew 3:13—4:11—His baptism and temptation experiences
both took place outdoors.
Matthew 14:23 and Luke 6:12—He often spent the night alone
in prayer on a hillside.
Matthew 5:1-20 and Luke 5:1-11—He often taught outdoors.
Matthew 8:23-27—He trusted God in a storm.

His teaching used illustrations taken from the outdoors:

Matthew 6:25-34—God's care for the things He created, the birds
and the flowers.
Matthew 13:1-9, 18-23—The sower.
Matthew 13:24-30, 36-43—The good seed and the bad seed.
Matthew 13:31-32—The mustard seed.
Matthew 16:1-3 and Luke 12:54-56—Knowing the signs of the sky.
Mark 4:26-29—God makes seeds to grow.
Luke 6:43-45—A good tree bears good fruit.

Luke 13:6-9 —The fig tree.
Luke 15:3-7 —The good shepherd.

(See additional Scripture references on pages 76, 100, 129.)

2. Stump Study

Stumps can tell quite a story to campers who take time to study them to find answers to such questions as the following:

1. How old was the tree when it was cut?
   One dark ring and one light ring make up one year's growth.
2. How was the tree cut? Which way did it fall?
   Look for clues in splinters left standing on the stump, for chips of wood or sawdust around the stump.
3. How long ago was the tree cut? Condition of stump and trees growing in the path of the tree's fall will give clues.
4. Was the tree ever injured by fire or drought?
5. How many years did it take to grow an inch in diameter in its best and worst years? What causes the difference in growth rate?
6. Why was the tree cut? Was it large enough for lumber? Was it thinned out?
7. How careful were the lumbermen? Consider amount of stump left, amount of top left, look for other trees injured in the felling process, and the condition of the area surrounding the stump.

3. Tree Key

Most people accept trees as part of the landscape and think very little about them. They are content to know a few by name. Trees become more interesting when we learn to identify them, and this is done by a study of their leaves, bark, buds, flowers, fruit, and growth habits. Sometimes it takes a skilled botanist to find the correct name. Tree keys have been developed to help us identify our trees. *How to Know the Trees,* by H. E. Jaques, is a good tree key book to use. An interesting project would be to develop a tree key for the trees found on your camp grounds and to make a book of leaf prints for the camp.

4. Nature Games

Reynold E. Carlson's *Nature Lore Manual for Church Leaders* gives excellent help on nature games and should be a camp resource book. A few ideas are given here for handy reference.

1. *Rocks and Leaves*
   The group is divided into two teams like "Flint" and "Oak." Each team has a leader who is the only one on the team able to pick up specimens spotted by teammates, who call him "Flint" or "Oak" as the case may be. At the end of a given time the

56

team with the most specimens wins. This game develops observation and acquaints the group with the objects involved.

2. *Tree Tag*

Three or four different kinds of trees are selected, such as oaks, hickories, and pines. The group is divided into as many teams as kinds of trees, with each camper standing by a tree, and one person as "It." When "It" calls the name of one kind of tree such as "Oak," all those campers must change places while he tries to get beside one of the trees. If "It" calls "Forest," everyone changes places. The person then left without a tree becomes "It."

3. *Matching Nature Objects*

Different kinds of leaves are cut in half. One half is given to a boy and the other half to a girl, but the pieces are mixed up so no one knows who has the other piece at the beginning of the game. At a signal the boys and girls try to match their pieces and to identify the leaf. First couple to do so wins. Game continues until all leaves are matched and identified. Other nature objects like sticks, bark, seeds, and sometimes rocks or shells can be used in place of the leaves.

4. *Trail Sentinel*

A group goes single file along a trail. First person stops near an object about which he can ask a question. Each camper whispers his answer so others cannot hear. If correct he may pass on; if wrong he must wait behind the sentinel until all campers have passed. The first camper to pass the sentinel becomes the new one and walks on until he finds something to stop and ask a question about.

5. *Games of Smell and Touch* (Good for nights or to play blindfolded during the day)

Identifying objects by smell—Good items are: pine, balsam, cedar, sassafras, mint, birch, wintergreen, pennyroyal, skunk cabbage, onion, sarsaparilla, apple, orange, tomato, humus.

Identifying objects by touch—Good items are: bark, leaves, fruits, vegetables, evergreens, some seeds, nuts, flowers, feathers, shells, and soils.

6. *Getting the Clue*

Have a sheet of paper with a hole in it. Show the edge of an object (leaf, rock, stick, etc.) a little more at a time. The first to guess correctly gets the object and the one to get the most wins.

7. *Nature Relays*

Have at opposite end of room several piles of scrambled natural objects. The leader of each relay team is given a list with as many items on it as there are players in line. At a signal, leader looks at first item on list, gives list to second player, and then goes to pile to get first object on list. When first returns

57

with correct object, second may go to claim second item on list, and so on down the line.

8. *Sharpen Your Senses*

Within a given area have campers list answers to:

(1) What colors can you find?
(2) What odors can you smell?
(3) What different trees do you see?
(4) What kinds of rocks can you find?
(5) What different plants can you find less than 2″ high?
(6) What kinds of homes can you find—animal, bird, and insect?
(7) What signs or tracks of animals, birds, or insects can you find?
(8) What sounds can you hear?
(9) Mark with a stick around your feet. What living things can you find in this marked-off area?

You have the idea! Make up your own questions or variations on these games.

CHAPTER 7

Relating the Camp Experience to the Home Situation

1. Pre-Camp Letters

To Campers

A camper should receive a prompt acknowledgment of his registration along with information concerning what to bring to camp and all other pertinent information. Usually a camper has previously received a camp publicity folder interpreting the camp program and telling how to get to camp. It is often wise to re-emphasize the importance of bringing sufficient blankets and rainwear for outdoor camping. The letter can also help the camper anticipate some of the experiences that await him and suggest he pray for God's help in making the most of the opportunity for Christian growth that lies ahead.

A suggested list of what to bring to camp would include the following:

4 sheets	Shorts, shirts, jeans
Pillow and 2 pillowcases	Bathing suit
3 blankets (one wool)	Sweater or jacket
Towels, washcloths	Raincoat, boots, hat
Soap	Rugged walking shoes
Toothbrush, toothpaste	Dress clothes for Sunday
Bible	2 or 3 pairs of pajamas
Stationery	Sleeping bag (if you have or can
Flashlight	borrow one)
Pocketknife	

To Parents

The letter to parents should seek to establish their confidence in the camp and its program; its provisions for the health and safety of campers at meals, on the waterfront, and through the services of a nurse in camp; the maturity and dedication of the counselors; and briefly what the camp experience can mean in the life of the camper. Some suggestions of ways in which the parents can help the campers prepare for their camp experience would be good—giving them a sense of

59

emancipation from the home, expecting them to have a good time and not get homesick, helping them know how to make up their bed and pack their own suitcase, and including in prayers at home petitions for the camper's coming experience. The letter should also state clearly the time and place of arrival (and if necessary the final payment of fees), the policy of no visitors in camp, and an invitation for parents to share in the closing service of worship immediately before the departure of campers.

To Ministers

The letter to the ministers of campers would be helpful if it stated briefly the purpose of the camp and included some specific suggestions of ways in which the local church can help prepare its young people for camp. Sunday school teachers and directors of Christian education can help through discussions, personal talks, and group programs. Some camps give suggestions for a "Commissioning Service" to be held in the church the Sunday before campers depart for camp, as a means of impressing on campers and church members alike the value of a church camping experience.

2. Follow-up Letters After Camp

To Campers

Campers are usually overjoyed to get a friendly, personal letter from their counselor shortly after camp, recalling some of their good times together as well as their most meaningful moments of worship or discussion. Such a letter can be a means of heightening the camper's resolve to continue his growth as a Christian at home and may come at a time when it is badly needed, during the "let-down" period many campers feel when they are no longer a part of the camp. Sometimes a counselor may wish to encourage a camper in specific areas of growth, and to sensitive Junior Highs it is done better through praise than through criticism.

Many counselors also like to remember their campers with a note at Christmas.

To Parents

Counselors often hesitate to write to parents but most parents deeply appreciate hearing from the counselor about how their child got along in camp. Such a letter need not be long. It could mention the good aspects of the camper's experience, with suggestions of ways in which the camper may be helped to carry on at home some of the things which seemed to mean much to him in camp, like times alone

60

for personal worship. Sometimes a counselor may wish to refer to some difficulty the camper may have had and the ways in which the camp experience seemed to help him. Parents appreciate being thanked by the counselor for the opportunity of having had their child in camp.

To the Minister

Most pastors appreciate a letter concerning their church young people who have been to camp. Many camps mimeograph a letter in which specific information about campers may be included, along with suggestions of ways in which the home church can help its campers use their experience for the benefit of the local church. Letters to pastors are particularly important in cases where a camper has expressed a desire to make a profession of faith when he returns home, or where problems have arisen with a camper, or where some unusual or particularly pertinent information needs to be conveyed for further help in the home situation.

Part III
THE THREEFOLD EMPHASIS FOR JUNIOR HIGH CAMPING

Use of the Threefold Emphasis

CHURCH CAMPING is an integral part of the total program of Christian education in our churches, and camping contributes unique learning opportunities that cannot be duplicated in the church or church school. Some things like church history or missions can be learned best in a classroom situation with a blackboard and resource materials. Other aspects of Christian experience like Christian community, Christian stewardship, and Christian growth in life situations can be learned best out of doors in close fellowship with God, His world, and other people, and in a situation where the experience is cumulative over a period of days. Camping in a setting where campers and counselors are consciously seeking to be Christian in all they do becomes an actual experience in a Christian community, where Christian growth is bound to take place in the persons involved, and where awareness of Christian stewardship grows naturally out of direct contact with and use of the resources of the natural world. This is learning through living: Christian growth as a Christian steward living in a small Christian community.

While the following three chapters develop these three aspects of Christian experience separately, such separation is quite arbitrary since these experiences cannot be wholly compartmentalized in the actual camping situation and learnings in all three areas will inevitably take place.

Why then the separation into three areas of emphasis? It is our conviction that leaders need a concept of what is involved in an understanding of Christian community, of Christian stewardship, and of Christian growth. Without such a sense of grasp of the ideas involved, many counselors feel lost and inadequate as leaders of their campers.

62

The following three chapters have been developed in such a way that counselors will have at their fingertips, not day by day programs, but an idea of where they are going and why in their living experiences, and of how to stimulate awarenesses in these areas through their camping activities. *The counselor in such a Christian camp program as this needs two sets of skills: he needs an understanding of what is involved in Christian Community, in Christian Stewardship, and in Christian Growth; and he needs a knowledge of campcraft as discussed in the preceding chapters, if he is to be an effective leader for his group.*

Some camps may wish to use this material in a three-year cycle plan with special emphasis placed on one of the three areas each year. In such camps this emphasis is undergirded with daily devotional material to stimulate the individual camper's awareness and understanding of God, intensified through the guidance of the counselor in daily camping activities and informal discussions. This devotional material gives campers a frame of reference for their daily living experiences that channels their thinking and interpretations more directly into the particular area of emphasis. Such a use of one of the following chapters is probably more intensive though necessarily more limited in scope.

Other camps prefer to make no emphasis beyond that of living together as Christians in a simple rustic setting in God's out-of-doors. In each small group, activities are planned out of the interests and needs of the group. Awareness of the Christian implications of their experience comes more spontaneously out of their own reactions to their experience. A mature Christian leader, conscious of a constant Christian frame of reference for all of life, also reacts in and to the group's experiences, and by sharing his thoughts—need we say informally—as friend and companion to his campers, he helps to stimulate their thinking and activity in Christian ways. Such a counselor has to be prepared to meet, handle, and contribute in situations where he may not be specifically prepared, so familiarity with the material in the following three chapters may form a helpful backlog of resources and guidance for him.

In either approach, the counselor will benefit tremendously in his preparation by using the "Counselor's Planning Section" in the back of the book to help in formulating his ideas and plans, and in making personal the material he needs for guidance from the chapters on "Christian Community," "Christian Stewardship," and "Christian Growth." Far more preparation is needed for guiding in as flexible a learning process as this, and a counselor needs to give a great deal of personal thought to what is involved in a Christian living experience in camp, to his own personal abilities, and to his campsite and campers.

Christian Community

Purposes of a Christian Community Emphasis

SMALL GROUP living in camp provides the church with an ideal situation in which to develop real Christian community. In this new situation among many new friends and guided by mature Christian counselors, boys and girls have the opportunity to give their best to the group and to put into practice the Christian concepts and attitudes they have discussed or only vaguely experienced in their home-church environment. In camp "the secret of a Christian group consciousness is the group's willingness to examine itself continually in the light of the principles and person of Christ and to reorder life accordingly."[1]

This is not to say, however, that Christian community will automatically develop in small group camping. A demanding and unsympathetic counselor, dictatorial in his ways and immature in his own personal growth as a Christian, will thwart the development of any feeling of Christian groupness. His means are undemocratic and his attitudes unchristlike. An unco-operative and selfish camper may hurt the development of a total feeling of community, but with mature Christian guidance on the part of the counselor the whole group can grow tremendously by seeking to provide the climate for a transforming experience in the life of that camper. Such struggling for Christian solutions to difficult problems often develops the most meaningful experience—that of a redeeming Christian fellowship.

64

But what is Christian community? What is it that we are seeking to experience with our campers?

The whole matter of salvation is tied up in God's calling of a community of believers into fellowship with Him and with each other, to be a means of communicating His gospel of redemption through the living example of such a redeeming fellowship.

The counselor will rightly want to know how this fellowship is developed in his small group, in his particular camp.

> If we are to walk in the *Spirit* our first lesson in the Spirit must be that we do not possess it but it possesses us. Better still, "He possesses us." *God is spirit,* and they who worship Him must worship Him in spirit and in truth. But if we are to be possessed by spirit we shall have to learn to give ourselves to Him; that means giving ourselves to this community. It means committing ourselves to one another in faith and trust. To walk in the spirit *here* is our faithfulness to one another before this altar and in the classroom and in play. It means that we trust and respect each other enough to speak the truth in love—which entails no diminishment of honesty or love. It means that we enter into one another's life and find at the heart of our common life that living, pulsing reality called the body of Christ. The amazing gift of Christian community is never manufactured in the individual, and one may possess it only by sharing it.[2]

All this takes place here and now, right where we are, in the common activities of camping, living in the light and power of God's love.

Thus when we seek to create in camp a foretaste of Christian community we begin with the small group in its everyday camping activities. We can never teach the meaning of Christian community by sitting down in a group to study it. That is an imitation experience, superficial, and vicarious. We experience Christian community by giving ourselves in the happy fellowship of a group busily working together preparing a cook-out supper after having resolved in a Christian way the conflicts of personalities that flared up among us; a group seeking to be aware of God at work in us and in our surroundings. In such a group, discussions around the embers of the campfire will deepen our perceptions of the work of the Spirit and our bonds of love toward one another.

By utilizing the camp activities that naturally appeal to Junior Highs—exploring, building a home of their own in the woods, cooking out, sleeping out, and many others—the capable counselor will find many opportunities to help the group discover itself as a group and to build fellowship and understanding among its individual members. In such a group periods of worship and prayer become vital, moments

65

of failure become springboards for spiritual strengthening, and the Bible becomes the Word of God speaking to their lives, *now*. The small group that develops a real Christian group consciousness is also the group that desires to reach out to share in the larger camp fellowship and beyond. One of the miracles of Christian love and fellowship is its need to go beyond itself, like the ripples on the surface of water when a pebble drops in.

With this idea of consciously seeking to create out of the fabric of daily camp life a Christian fellowship that will be a living witness to a real and vibrant love, drawing all whom it touches into a deeper fellowship with Christ, let us consider four specific purposes that help in our understanding of the development of Christian community. Briefly stated they are these:

1. To provide an experience in Christian group living—an experience in the redeemed and redeeming community.
2. To help the campers find themselves in relation to others for the welfare of all.
3. To help the group learn to resolve conflicts and handle difficulties in a Christlike manner.
4. To provide opportunity for the small group to share with the larger camp group and beyond.

Ways of Achieving These Purposes Through Camp Activities

A. *To provide an experience in Christian group living—an experience in the redeemed and the redeeming community.*

Campers and leaders are like disciples being led by Christ's Spirit, becoming One Body in Christ, constantly seeking to develop a feeling of fellowship with Him and with each other and trying to carry out all activities in the spirit of Christian love. Or we could put it this way: God has called me to live as His in this group now. I am seeking to carry out His will by giving myself wholeheartedly to this group where I am.

> —Christ and His principles become the point of reference as the group seeks to make their life together more Christian. In discussions: What would Jesus do? In handling this problem? In making this decision? Where have we failed? How could we have done better?

> —Through the Bible, God confronts the group with the revelation of His will for Christian community—our community—now!

66

—Prayer becomes a vital means of binding the group closer to God and to each other.

—All activities are *means* through which a deeper awareness of the meaning of Christian fellowship is developed—exploration and discovery, work, worship, and play. The following activities, indigenous to camp, are ones through which Christian community can develop.

1. *Explorations and Discovery*

   (1) Take orientation and exploration hikes around the camp area, perhaps with a view toward co-operatively developing their home-in-the-woods.

   (2) Share observations and discoveries of rocks, weather, trees, plants, birds, and animals with your own group, and with the total camp through a nature shelf or bulletin board. Collect samples of wood, rocks, old nests, interesting plants, etc., for sharing. Discover land formations, glacial terrain, types of soil, rock formations, effects of erosion, lakes, and swamps, and plan to share information and discoveries.

   (3) Take compass trips, sharing in reading the compass and following the azimuth together. Observe positions of land and rock formations on the way. For older Junior Highs a night compass hike by flashlight can be extra fun if done over a relatively easy course.

   (4) Include cooking out and/or camping out overnight on an exploration trip. This involves additional co-operation and sharing of responsibilities to prepare for all the essentials, and to carry them out successfully.

   (5) Key trees *together* to learn how to recognize different trees and families of trees.

   (6) Follow animal trails together, sharing findings and perhaps making plaster casts of tracks to share with other groups.

   (7) Study stumps. A group can have a world of fun piecing together the history of a tree from the different clues they discover in its stump.

   (8) Take a rainy-day hike together to enjoy the rain and observe its effects on the land. Smell it, too!

   (9) Mark with stones or stakes a trail to some special spot to share with others.

   (10) Lay a "treasure hunt" trail for sharing with another small group.

   (11) Take fishing trips together. Share responsibilities for getting equipment and bait and enjoy cooking "the catch" too.

   (12) Take trips as a group along a beach or lake shore, observing, collecting, noticing erosion and effects on soil and rocks. Share findings with others back in camp.

67

(13) Take trips together by boat on lake or other body of water.

(14) Take mountain trips, being considerate of those in group who climb more slowly.

(15) Take special trips to gather materials for group craft work: grasses and reeds for weaving; clay, driftwood, sassafras, cedar, pods, and pine cones for craft work, etc.

(16) Take special trips for gathering wild foods such as berries, salad greens, and sassafras roots and mint leaves for tea.

(17) Go trip camping to a special place the distance of one or more days from camp. Plan for food, clothes, shelter, and first-aid. Take time to see things on the way.

(18) Take night trips together—a moonlight hike, a star-gaze on a hilltop or in a boat on a lake. (How close can the stars get!) Notice night animals on the way.

(19) Go on fossil and arrowhead hunting trips, seeking information together, talking with "old timers" of the neighborhood, developing an awareness of one's heritage. Share findings with larger camp group through nature shelf, or even through a dramatic skit at a campfire some night.

(20) Make weather observations to gain a knowledge of instruments and their use, to recognize weather signs and symbols, and use observations in daily forecasting. Keep records. If none exists, help make a weather station for the camp.

2. Cook-outs

Plan for a meal to be prepared, cooked, and eaten out of doors, with specific clean-up responsibilities assigned. Menus can range from simple pow-wow refreshments or a breakfast, through lunches and dinners, to progressive meals in which each co-operating small group is responsible for preparing and serving one course of the meal. Co-operation and sharing of responsibilities are learned as each camper seeks to do his part as a respected member of his group. Cook-outs on the trail challenge older Junior Highs to plan wisely and to carry out responsibilities. (You can't run back to camp for salt if you forget it!)

3. Campcraft

(1) Build a home-in-the-woods with fireplace, lashed tables, benches, etc. (See chapter 3, "Campcraft," in Part II.)

(2) Construct hogans or other shelter for a group.

(3) Build foot bridges, rustic signs and markers, check-dams for erosion control, or other camp service projects for the benefit of others besides one's own group.

(4) Carve wooden articles—knives, ladles, spoons, weather vanes, bowls, sculptured pieces, book ends, candle holders, and other items useful in the small group campsite.

(5) Enjoy clay work, making bowls, hot dish tiles, etc.

(6) Weave baskets, table mats, and trays out of reeds, honey-

suckle, grasses, sassafras splints, or willow shoots. Dye with natural dyes made from boiled berries, walnut hulls, onion skins, etc. (See chapter 4, "Use of Creative Activities," in Part II.)

(7) Make rustic bird baths and feeding stations for birds and small animals near the group's campsite.

4. *Worship*

(1) Plan periods for individual and for group worship.
Individual—morning watch, times during the day for meditation, bedtime devotional opportunities.
Corporate—small group vespers, special worship services, dedication services, Sunday worship. Individual worship undergirds group worship and group worship deepens private meditation.

(2) Be on the alert for moments of worship in response to the group's unfolding awareness of God—when discovering something of particular beauty in nature, when feeling the coolness of a refreshing rain, when wondering at the magnitude of creation at a star-gaze, or when experiencing the joy of friendship in a job well done together.

(3) Write litanies, poems, and prayers that grow out of the group experience. These may be used as part of a corporate worship experience.

(4) Enjoy a group hymn sing in some lovely spot, or an echo sing across a lake or from hill to hill. The first can be spontaneous; the latter must be planned in advance and can include a larger camp group.

(5) Dramatize a particularly meaningful passage of Scripture, working out ideas and acting together, and perhaps plan to share it with a larger camp group. Some suggestions are:

Acts 10 where God reveals to Peter that no man is common or unclean. Perhaps add a contemporary episode.

I Corinthians 12—Different gifts but all members of the Body of Christ.

Acts 12:1-17—The power of prayer in releasing Peter from prison.

A dramatization of the covenant relationship from Abraham, through Christ, to us.

A dramatization of the story "Where Love Is," found in resource section of this chapter.

5. *Discussions*

(1) Plan activities, seek to solve special problems, share discoveries, and summarize ideas through discussions.

(2) Share the use of resources such as the Bible, other books, and persons of special ability, as a means of deepening insights and understandings in discussions.

(3) Evaluate activities and attitudes.

69

(4) Use role-playing as a means of aiding discussion.

(5) Encourage conversations among two or three, or a "bull session" or "pow-wow" in the small group, as a wonderful opportunity to help individuals and the group to grow in understanding.

6. *Rest and Quiet Times*

In a group where real rapport exists, periods of rest and quiet are recognized as needed periods of real re-creation and study, and even help to draw a group closer together. Sleep, quiet times of meditation, siesta, observation of wild life, and the like bind a group closer in fellowship.

7. *Evening Activities*

(1) Enjoy campfires!

Small group pow-wows for informal discussions, evaluation, planning, *and fun* around the campfire.

Fun campfires, consisting of songs, stories, "tall tales," games, by small group or larger camp group.

Campfire for worship service, using hymns, spirituals, drama, stories, prayer, and dedication, by small group or larger camp group.

(2) Enjoy an echo sing between groups.

(3) Have an evening of folk games and/or charades and other games with whole camp group, or two or three small groups together. A progressive game night provides different activities in different locations, and groups move progressively through them at specified times during the evening. Include folk games, storytelling, charades, active games, etc. This could be a co-operative venture wherein each small group provides one part of the program, either at its own campsite or home-in-the-woods, or in some more central location.

(4) Enjoy a night hike or a star-gaze as a group, sharing observations and feelings and the pure fun of doing it together.

(5) Have a sleep-out. It takes a heap of co-operation to fix sleeping areas that are comfortable and safe.

8. *Camp Chores and Care of Camp Property*

(1) Share dining hall responsibilities, going the extra mile beyond duty by fixing pretty centerpieces and sharing the joy of having done something especially nice for the pleasure of others.

(2) Keep the shelter clean and in order out of a genuine concern for the welfare of others instead of through the false stimulation of inspections and awards. Each person does his share, and more!

(3) Carry out other camp chores such as cleaning latrines, bathhouses, craft area, etc. (if these are part of the campers'

70

responsibility), with the same loving concern for the welfare of others. Carry this into a considerate use of these common areas.

(4) Develop a genuine concern for others and their needs by carefully using and returning in good condition all camp property such as tools, special cooking equipment, boats, books, weather instruments, and small group equipment.

9. *Play Times*

(1) Share spontaneous moments of play for the sheer joy of enjoying our companions—an outpouring of ourselves in love and fun.

(2) Play games together along the trail, as a break in small group activities or discussion times.

(3) Go swimming and boating together. Share fun and skills. Help a new camper to learn to swim or improve his stroke, or to learn boating.

B. *To help the campers find themselves in relation to others for the welfare of all.*

1. *To be accepted as part of the group*

The dominant drive of Junior Highs is to be accepted and appreciated as part of the group. Their whole world is expanding before them. They are allowed more freedom to decide their own courses of action, and part of the feeling of security given them by their parents is now achieved through a sense of security in the group. This is a difficult growing time—physically, socially, and psychologically.

Co-ed camping is also a means of restoring boy-girl relationships to a natural foundation of mutual respect and understanding through common activities, overcoming the artificialities of such relationships often imposed on young minds by movies and T.V. This is a more mature acceptance of each other based on individual worth.

2. *Opportunity to be a person in his own right*

In small group camping the individual is given a constant opportunity to be a person in his own right. The camper is free from parental control and such freedom is valuable for the development of his initiative, resourcefulness, and sense of responsibility to the group. The small group makes possible the climate for the sharing of individual personality. Each camper finds it necessary to take part in group decisions, formulating ideas,

71

carrying out activities, and evaluating actions. He becomes involved in purposes and activities apparently beyond himself, drawing on and developing his inner resources and self-control, and giving even that which he is just finding. What he has to give is accepted by the group because it is needed, provided it is an honest expression of himself. Such intimate group living requires personal honesty; the braggart is shown for what he really is and is led to overcome his difficulty, the shy person is drawn out in an openly friendly situation, the more capable ones help the others, and the feeling of mutual dependence on one another helps to bring out the best in each.

Everything done in camp can be a means of fulfilling this purpose. Casual discussions in the bath house, or after lights-out, are as important as the more directed discussions within the small group. The attitude of a counselor toward a problem raised by a camper may have a more lasting effect on the group than all else he says or does. The manner in which many decisions are made may be of more importance than the actual decision made so far as the growth of the campers, individually and as a group, is concerned.

3. *Through group planning*

Small group camping means self-determination to quite a full extent. Within the bounds of the camp and its agreed-upon schedule for such things as bedtime, mealtimes, and chores, campers are quite free to develop their own program together with other campers under the guidance of wise and friendly counselors. Such group decisions are made first in the small group and then in the larger camp family as the need and desire for fuller participation and sharing arises.

In determining their program a small group is guided by the interests of its individual members. Sometime during the first afternoon or evening a counselor can lead the group into a discussion of "What would you like to do in camp?" Such a casual, though directed question stimulates the group into the beginning of their own program planning led by their own interests. Of course, the counselor will want to add suggestions of other activities that the campers have not thought about, to help them broaden their own vision of things that are possible in the camp and fascinating to do, and that will help the group achieve real Christian community.

The individual finds himself a controlling element in the

democratic procedure, but he will not be able to dominate the group any more than the group will completely control him. In every democratic organization the individual, unique in his ability and personality, must be respected as much as is a larger minority viewpoint. Sometimes Christian love encourages the "bending over backward" of the majority will to that of a steadfast minority. Here Christian love vitally determines the relationship.

4. *Self-discipline*

Discipline in the small group generally grows out of the inner desires of the individual rather than being imposed from without. When a feeling of group rapport is developing, each camper, in an effort to keep his status within the group, is sensitive to the need for personal self control so that the group can accomplish its plans without friction. Thus, rest time is better respected in small group camping because the campers recognize the need for rest in order to carry on their work. When a member of the group fails to exhibit self control and the spirit of co-operation, the campers themselves often seek to bring that camper back into the total fellowship of the group. The wise counselor will want to help the group in such efforts as well as to seek an understanding with the camper himself. Once again, Christian love should be the motivating factor.

C. *To help the group learn to resolve conflicts and handle difficulties in a Christlike manner.*

1. *The redeeming community*

While small group camping provides exceptional opportunities for the growth of real Christian fellowship, we must realize that the close living situation can also heighten conflict. Here is the rub, literally, for the closer people live together the greater their conflicts can become. This is seen in some homes where personalities irritate each other in constant daily contact, and it is also the marvel of homes that have surmounted difficulties and achieved an enviable unity.

Every group starting out on a new adventure in camp has potentialities for good—and possibilities for difficulty since no one is perfect. The group is primarily dependent upon the wise and mature Christian leadership of its counselor to guide it into a sense of being a redeeming community. Campers need guidance

73

in learning to "overcome evil with good," in becoming "reconciled with their brother," in "bearing one another's burdens," and in experiencing a sense of being forgiven as well as becoming capable of forgiving. The counselor guides by leading the group into an awareness of God working His redeeming love through them. A consciousness of Christian community, of the fellowship of love, can be most meaningful here in the area of resolving conflicts in Christ's way, and the group that has surmounted such difficulty together has grown stronger for the experience.

2. *Prayer*

Prayer—directed silent prayer or spoken group prayer—can be the quiet that calms and allows God to guide. John R. Mott used to stop discussion when it got heated and have prayer, and counselors may find this an effective way of giving the group time to calm down and grow more objective and peaceful. Bible study of particularly relevant passages is most helpful to a group seeking to find its way through a problem. The counselor will want to lead the campers in a search for their own answers rather than "preaching" to them.

One of the first steps in overcoming difficulty is to realize that none of us is without sin, and that when we seek to effect reconciliation it must be in the spirit of mutual need and helpfulness. We must let God work through us, and sometimes we must learn to let go, to yield our anxiety over a problem to Him, and to carry on our activities as joyously as possible in spite of difficulty.

3. *Handling disappointments*

Disappointments happen in camp and can cause real group difficulties. What does a group do when rain settles in for days and all the group's wonderful plans for a two-day mountain trip are literally washed away? Can they muster enough ingenuity and will-power to stretch a tarp between trees at their campsite to shelter them while they lash their tables and build their fireplace, as one group did? Campers' stew and hot cocoa never tasted better than out there under the tarp in the rain! And later, when the sun finally shone, the group took off on the trip they'd planned and had their nice campsite as well. Another group had not planned much craft work but turned to it when rain spoiled other plans. Later, a camper commented, "Just think, if it hadn't rained we would only have worked on our campsite, and now we got to do crafts as well."

74

There was another group who had planned to do some extensive exploring and found themselves faced with the problem of a camper who had sprained his ankle and couldn't go hiking. After much honest discussion they decided on a happy revision of activities that included him.

One camp had no swimming because the lack of rain had cut the water supply in their small natural lake. The leaders feared real trouble from disappointed campers who naturally, in such hot dry weather, would enjoy a good swim. Much to their surprise they found that the campers responded to the challenge and stronger group fellowship developed through day-long activities at their campsites and on trips uninterrupted by breaks for swimming.

4. *Learning to live with people who are different*

Actually having the experience of living with people who are different—those with physical handicaps, or of different racial, economic, social, and cultural backgrounds—dispels more fear, mistrust, and false ideas than all the discussions in the world. And no camp can call itself "Christian" and be exclusive in any sense of the word. Jesus said, "If you love those who love you, what reward have you? Do not even the tax collectors do the same? And if you salute only your brethren, what more are you doing than others? . . . You, therefore, must be perfect, as your heavenly Father is perfect." (Matthew 5:46-48, R.S.V.)

Living with those who seem different to us, and learning to know and understand them and to love them, also

—makes us realize we have more similarities than differences.

—makes us aware of personality rather than outward appearance of color, dialect, clothes, or physical condition. Jesus looked into a person and dealt with personality. Can we do less and call ourselves Christian?

—heightens our appreciation for their special contributions to group life: songs, stories, customs.

Such understanding and appreciation can lead to a desire to share with others beyond the camp group in gifts, plans for further fellowship, or means of helping and sharing our Christian concern for their welfare.

D. *To provide opportunity for the small group to share with the larger camp group and beyond.*

The small group that develops a joyous Christian group

75

consciousness finds itself desiring to reach out and share the good it has found with other groups in camp, and in time to extend its fellowship beyond the camp family. It is probably wise to seek to develop some sense of groupness in the small group before planning activities involving other groups or the whole camp.

Some ways of sharing between groups are the following:

1. *Cook-outs* in which the small group entertains another group.
2. *Progressive dinners* in which the various small groups involved, usually three, prepare the appetizer, the main course, or the dessert at their own campsites, and then leave one or two campers to watch the food while the rest of the group joins the others at the campsite where the first course is being served at a time agreed upon. The groups then "progress" from one campsite to the next for the parts of the meal contributed by each group.
3. *Fun campfires* with each group helping with songs, stories, charades, etc.
4. *Vesper services* and hymn sings with other groups. In such vesper services there can be planned sharing of litanies, poems, and meditations that have grown out of the different small group experiences.
5. *Game nights* with the whole camp together for folk games, charades, and storytelling, or with one small group moving from one activity to another during the course of the evening. Various skilled leaders are drawn from their small groups leaving their co-counselor in charge of their group while they lead in folk games, storytelling, or active games.
6. *Sunday worship,* often a whole camp activity, in which the various small groups participate. In other camps one small group is responsible for planning the complete service to be shared with the whole camp.

The Sunday offering is a means of sharing with the larger world community. Suggestions and discussions concerning particular needs or projects can be carried on in the small groups, and the final vote on where the offering should go can be made by the whole camp group.

Helpful Scripture Passages

1. An Experience in the Redeemed and Redeeming Community

Experiencing Christian Community Through Worship

Matthew 18:19-20—Where two or three are gathered in my name.
John 4:23-24—True worship.

The Covenant Between God and His People

Genesis 17:7-9—God's covenant with Abraham and his descendants.
Exodus 6:2-8—God reaffirms the covenant to Moses.
Exodus 20:1-17—The Ten Commandments.

Micah 6:8—What does the Lord require of you?
Luke 2:25-32—Simeon's prophecy concerning Christ.
Luke 3:15-16—John's prophecy concerning Jesus.
Luke 4:1-2a, 14-21—Jesus begins His ministry, in the Spirit.
John 3:16-21—For God so loved the world.
John 10:14-18—One shepherd, one flock (The Good Shepherd).
John 14:6-15—Jesus reveals the Father by doing His will.
John 17:20-26—Jesus' prayer that they may all be one.
Matthew 26:36-46—Jesus in Gethsemane—"Thy will be done."
John 14:12-14, 25-26—Jesus' promise of the coming of the Holy
               Spirit.
Acts 2:38-39—The promise of the Holy Spirit.
Revelation 21:1-4—John's vision of the new heaven and earth.

Early Christian Community

Acts 2:44-47—The first Christian community.
Acts 4:32-37—The first Christian community.
Acts 12:12-17—The power of prayer in the Christian community.
Romans 1:11-12—Mutually encouraged by each other's faith.
Galatians 6:9-10—Do good . . . especially to those who are of the
               household of faith.
I John—all of it!—A fine expression of Christian community.
I Peter 2:9-10—God's people.
I Peter 3:8-12—Love of the brethren.
I Thessalonians 5:12-24—Encourage each other.
II Corinthians 13:5-9—Examine yourselves—Hold the faith.

2. Campers Finding Themselves in Relation to Others

Love and the Christian Community

Matthew 22:37-40—The two great commandments.
Colossians 3:12-17—The Christian community.
I Corinthians 12:4—13:13—Members of the Body of Christ united
               through love. (Ch. 13 is the beloved
               "Love" chapter.)
Romans 12—Members of the Christian community and how they
               live in it.
Luke 6:27-36—The Golden Rule.
John 13:34-35—Love one another.
John 15:12-17—The commandment to love one another.
Romans 13:8-10—Love your neighbor.
I John 3:11-18—Not love in word but in deed.
I John 4:7-21—He who loves God loves his brother.
James 2:14-17—Live your faith.

Working Together

Romans 12:1-12—Having gifts that differ—use them!
Philippians 2:1-8—Look to the interests of others.
Nehemiah 1, 2, 4—Working together to rebuild the city walls.

3. Handling Difficulties in a Christlike Manner

Learning to Handle Difficulty and Conflict

Exodus 20:16—Do not bear false witness.
Exodus 20:17—Do not covet.
Matthew 5:21-24—Be reconciled with your brother, then worship.
Matthew 7:1-5—Judge not, that ye be not judged.
Matthew 18:15-17—Seek a reconciliation with one who sins.
Matthew 18:21-22—How often shall I forgive?
Luke 22:24-27—True greatness.
John 8:2-11—He who is without sin, cast the first stone.
John 13:12-17—Jesus washing disciples' feet.
Romans 12:14-21—Overcome evil with good.
Romans 14:10-13—Let us not pass judgment, nor be a hindrance.
Galatians 6:1-2—Bear one another's burdens.
Ephesians 4:25-32—Control evil as members one of another.
Colossians 3:12-17—How the Christian community handles conflict.
James 2:1-9—Do not show partiality.
James 4:11-12—Do not speak evil of a neighbor.
I Peter 3:8-9—Do not return evil for evil.
I John 2:9-11 and 4:20—Do not have hatred in your heart.

Living with People Who Are Different

John 4:5-15—Jesus and the Samaritan woman.
Acts 10 or 11:4-18—God reveals to Peter that no man is common or unclean. (Verses 10:28, 34-35 especially good.)
Acts 17:26—Made from one every nation on the earth.
Romans 10—Concerning getting along with people who believe differently. (Especially verses 10-13.)

4. Serving Others in the Larger World Community

Matthew 19:16-22—The rich young ruler—Go, give, come . . .
Matthew 25:34-45—Caring for the hungry, thirsty, the strangers. "Inasmuch as ye have done it unto one of the least of these."
Matthew 28:19-20—Go ye into all the world . . .
Acts 11:26-30—Early Christians send relief contributions.

Hymns Particularly Appropriate for Christian Community Emphasis

We Would Be Building; Temples Still Undone
Dear Lord and Father of Mankind
For the Beauty of the Earth (Especially stanza 3)
In Christ There is No East or West
Now in the Days of Youth
Blest Be the Tie That Binds
When Thy Heart with Joy O'erflowing
O Brother Man, Fold to Thy Heart Thy Brother
At Length There Dawns the Glorious Day
Hail the Glorious Golden City

78

Faith of Our Fathers, Living Still
Where Cross the Crowded Ways of Life
The Light of God Is Falling
Come, Let Us Join with Faithful Souls
Teach Us, O Lord, True Brotherhood
I Bind My Heart This Tide
Turn Back, O Man
Let There Be Light, Lord God of Hosts
O Master, Let Me Walk with Thee
Take Thou Our Minds, Dear Lord
The Church's One Foundation
O Young and Fearless Prophet
Joyful, Joyful, We Adore Thee
The Voice of God Is Calling

Resources in Prose and Poetry

BRIEF ILLUSTRATIONS

Prejudice

"Prejudice is our method of transferring our own sickness to others. It is our ruse for disliking others rather than ourselves. . . . Prejudice is a raft onto which the shipwrecked mind clambers and paddles to safety."[1]

—Ben Hecht

"You can't hold a man down without staying down with him."

—Booker T. Washington

Or said another way—"You can't fence another man out without fencing yourself in."

Parable of the Piano[2]

"You can play some sort of tune on the white keys of a piano; you can play some sort of tune on the black keys; but to produce real harmony you must play both the black and the white keys."

—J. E. Kwegyir Aggrey, a native African teacher.

Each for All[3]

One group had used the slogan "Each for All" in achieving brotherly relations in the camp community. One morning, a certain boy who was most enthusiastic about swimming was seen sitting under a tree at swim time although he had continually pestered the counselors with, "When can we swim?" A counselor could not understand why he was not in the water. His question, "Aren't you feeling well?" brought a noncommittal answer.

Finally the counselor saw another boy, a very poor swimmer,

diving awkwardly in a pair of bright trunks that looked familiar. "That's So-and-so in swimming, isn't it?" he asked. "He's doing pretty well for a beginner." "Yes!" said the boy. "He's got a pair of trunks like yours." "Aw," said the boy, "they are mine. He didn't have any and he wasn't having any fun. I didn't want to go in today and I told him to take mine." Then, with a twinkle, "Each for all, you know."

—L. B. Hazzard

Gossip Illustration [4]

There is a familiar story told of a noted village gossip whose minister asked her to bring him a feather pillow. When she brought it to him he cut a small hole in one corner and told her to carry it back home. By the time she reached her house most of the feathers had come out. Her minister suggested that she go back and pick them up. "You know that's impossible on a windy day like this," she replied. "Well," said the minister, "that's exactly what happens when you spread idle gossip about your neighbors. You never can take back what you have said even if you want to."

"He who forgives ends the quarrel."—African proverb.

"The best way to get even is to forget."—Anonymous.

The glory of Friendship is not the outstretched hand, nor the kindly smile, nor the joy of companionship; it is the spiritual inspiration that comes to one when he discovers that someone else believes in him and is willing to trust him with his friendship.

—Selected

My friends have come to me unsought. The great God gave them to me.—Ralph Waldo Emerson (Essay on Friendship)

POETRY

The Search

No one could tell me what my soul might be;
I searched for God, and He eluded me;
I sought my brother out, and found all three.
—Ernest H. Crosby (1856-1907)

A Prayer [5]

Make me too brave to lie or be unkind.
Make me too understanding, too, to mind
The little hurts companions give, and friends,
The careless hurts that no one quite intends.
Make me too thoughtful to hurt others so.
Help me to know
The inmost hearts of those for whom I care,
Their secret wishes, all the loads they bear,
That I may add my courage to their own.
May I make lonely folks feel less alone

80

And happy ones a little happier yet.
May I forget
What ought to be forgotten; and recall
Unfailingly, all
That ought to be recalled, each kindly thing,
Forgetting what might sting.
To all upon my way,
Day after day,
Let me be joy, be hope! Let my life sing!

—Mary Carolyn Davies

The Search[6]

I sought His love in sun and stars,
  And where the wild seas roll,
And found it not. As mute I stood,
  Fear overwhelmed my soul;
But when I gave to one in need,
I found the Lord of Love indeed.

I sought His love in lore of books,
  In charts of science' skill;
They left me orphaned as before—
  His love eluded still;
Then in despair I breathed a prayer;
The Lord of Love was standing there!

—Thomas Curtis Clark

Awareness[7]

God—let me be aware.
Stab my soul fiercely with others' pain,
Let me walk seeing horror and stain.
Let my hands, groping, find other hands.
Give me the heart that divines, understands.
Give me the courage, wounded, to fight.
Flood me with knowledge, drench me in light.
Please—keep me eager just to do my share.
God—let me be aware.

—Miriam Teichner

God's Dreams[8]

Dreams are they—but they are God's dreams!
Shall we decry them and scorn them?
That men shall love one another,
That white shall call black man brother,
That greed shall pass from the market place,
That lust shall yield to love for the race,
That man shall meet with God face to face—
Dreams are they all,
    But shall we despise them—
    God's dreams!

81

Dreams are they—to become man's dreams!
Can we say nay as they claim us?
That men shall cease from their hating,
That war shall soon be abating,
That the glory of kings and lords shall pale,
That the pride of dominion and power shall fail,
That the love of humanity shall prevail—
Dreams are they all,
But shall we despise them—
God's dreams!

—Thomas Curtis Clark

If I knew you and you knew me:
If both of us could clearly see,
And, with an inner light, divine
The meaning of your heart and mine,
I'm sure that we should suffer less,
And clasp our hands in friendliness;
Our thoughts would pleasantly agree,
If I knew you and you knew me.

—Author unknown

A Creed[9]

There is a destiny that makes us brothers;
None goes his way alone:
All that we send into the lives of others
Comes back into our own.

—Edwin Markham

Outwitted

He drew a circle that shut me out—
Heretic, rebel, a thing to flout.
But Love and I had the wit to win:
We drew a circle that took him in!

—Edwin Markham

STORIES

The Church That Was Builded by Moonlight[10]

There was rejoicing in the little village of India. The last load of clay had been brought to the trampling ground and mixed with the right amount of straw and water. As the plain around the village turned golden with the rays of the setting sun striking through the dust, the last brick was molded and set to dry.

The small boys of the Christian community played tag among the neat piles of brick. The women paused on their way from the well to see if the word was true that the last brick had been

82

molded. The young men were checking the count to make sure that there were indeed enough.

Raj-Singh, the preacher-teacher, was talking eagerly to the older men. "The ground is bought. The bricks are made. Now in just a few weeks we shall have our place of worship complete!"

It was a very simple place of worship they were planning. Just a floor of beaten earth, with a low brick wall around it to keep out cattle and dogs. The wall would be made with the bricks set wide apart like a lattice to let the stray breezes come through. At one end would be a higher wall rising to a peak.

"That wall we will make solid," said Raj-Singh, "and in it we will leave little openings in the brickwork, so that light will shine through to form the shape of a cross. Thus we shall ever have before us the symbol of our Christian faith. And thus everyone will know that it is a house of Christian praise."

Everyone rejoiced. They hoped to have their place of worship finished by the end of the month.

But there was trouble waiting for them in the village. The Hindu landlord and the priest of the Hindu temple did not want a Christian place of worship in their village.

"These Christians will attract others to their teachings," muttered the priest, "and the worship of our own gods Shiv and Vishnu will be neglected. Let us forbid the building of that place of worship. Then they will not be able to worship their God."

The landlord agreed. He went to Raj-Singh and the Christian elders. He did not discuss the matter with them. He simply said, "There will be no Christian place of worship built. It is my order. If any building is done, I will have my young men tear down each night that which is built each day. Save yourselves the trouble."

Alas and alas! All the rejoicing was turned to sorrow. The last-made bricks were neatly piled up with the others, and no one moved a hand to the building. For of what use was it to have the bricks ruined by being hacked down with pickaxes after they had been formed into walls?

Only Raj-Singh was thoughtful. "Have patience," he said. "We have a right to our place of worship, and there must be some way by which we can lawfully build it."

Raj-Singh went to town and talked to those who knew the law. He found that there was nothing to keep the landlord from destroying their work.

Raj-Singh went to another town. The Christian people there were interested. They looked among the laws of the land. They found a law which suited the situation. It said, "If a place of worship is erected and standing, no one may tear it down. But it must be finished before the protection of the law is upon it."

Raj-Singh went home. He gathered the Christian elders and told them about that one law. "I do not know how we can protect our place of worship while it is yet building and not finished," he ended sadly.

There was silence for a while. So deep was the thought that the faint rustle of a snake, going about his business in the hedgerow, could be heard. Then an old man spoke.

"There is a way," he said. "But who shall make it succeed? To carry it out, we would need to be more secret than the snake in the grass and more busy than Sher Khan the tiger when he hunts his food, and wise as the ant-folk who have a task for each and keep each one working every minute."

"Tell us the plan," begged the elders.

"It is this," said the Old One. "There will come a night when the moon is full and rises after the village is abed. We Christians will put out our lights and seem to go to bed also, but soon we will rise. Silently as the jackal we must slink along in the shadows till the walls of the village are behind us. Then, with the moon to light us, and in silence, we must work. Men and women and children, we must work by the light of the moon."

Raj-Singh snapped his fingers in delight. "Wise words! Wise words!" he said. But his voice he kept low, so that no passing villager might hear and tell. "Old One, our planning shall be done with the wisdom of the ant-folk. No person shall be idle but all shall work at one part or another of the brickwork. By the time the moon sinks to its rest and the stars fade out, the building will be done!"

The elders, skilled in the use of bricks, talked long and earnestly. They decided who should tramp down the floor. They planned how the bricks should be carried and laid loosely in place by the women and the children. They agreed that the best builders among them should lay the first course, and after that how the best builders would work on different parts of the wall. Each builder would have a group of women and children and older lads to help with brick and mud plaster.

Like the ant-folk they planned. They thought that the women and the little children might get weary, after the first rush of work was done. So they arranged for some to sit and rest while others worked. But for each there was a task and a place and a time to work.

They did not rush their planning. Best that the village should think they had given it up. Yet with every passing day the plans became more perfect.

One by one the Christians learned about it. But never a word slipped from their lips.

The old Hindu priest and the Hindu landlord laughed to themselves. "They are afraid!" they said. "They have no courage to go forward with their building."

But the moon became fuller and fuller. The night finally arrived when out of a clear sky the moon and a million stars shone down upon the earth with a light almost as bright as the sun. Only the shadows were black like velvet and the Hindu people of the village went early to bed, to be ready to go to a near-by fair at break of day.

When silence lay upon the village, the Christians rose and

stole like shadows out into the night. Mothers and fathers and little children; older boys and girls, eager and excited; young men and old, all were ready to work through the night to build their place of worship.

Truly, it was like a colony of the ant-people. Almost in silence, except for whispered questions and answers, the Christians worked.

Almost like magic, that floor of earth, spreading like a pool of water in the moonlight, stretched itself out, under the trampling feet of the workers, till it reached the measured boundary of the walls. Almost like magic the first course of brick was laid in the four walls around the floor.

Then the walls began to rise. Slowly but surely, while the blazing stars swung overhead, and the moon rode the heavens from east to west.

The little children grew weary and slept upon the blankets their mothers had laid along the edge of the field. The older boys and girls grew tired, but they worked doggedly on. The mothers took turns, guarding the babies for a while and then working. They carried water to the men-folk and helped through the breathless, hot night.

One man finished his work, and straightening, stretched his arms toward the stars. Another and another followed. They gathered about the west wall, where the cross had been made, with openwork in the brick. At last only one man worked on, laying the bricks in the peak of the wall. The light of the lowering moon shone through the cross, and its pattern lay in light amid the black shadows on the new tramped floor.

Then the people gathered into their place of worship, and sat in orderly rows upon the still damp earth. The mothers carried the sleeping little ones that later they, too, might say, "We were there."

Raj-Singh lifted up his arms and the heads of the people bowed in prayer. They did not notice that dawn, swift tropical dawn, had come and that the astonished Hindus stood at the edge of the field.

Raj-Singh lifted up his voice. He prayed the first prayer in the new house of worship. He prayed earnestly and mightily and with great love for God.

Then he turned to see the landlord and the Hindu priest, who said, "What have you done?"

Raj-Singh answered simply, "We have built a house of worship for our God." He looked the landlord straight in the eye.

The landlord shrugged his shoulder. "I was fearful," he said, "of just one thing. I was afraid you might find out about that law. Even so, no idea came into my head that you might so greatly desire a house of God that you would work thus all night."

The landlord looked at the trodden floor and the latticed walls and the cross in the western wall. "Be secure," he said. "Be secure in your house of worship." He raised his voice. "The hand of no man shall be lifted to move one brick from the wall, or to injure in any way this house of worship. It is the law," said the landlord.

85

The Christian folk raised a shout of joy. They were weary and their eyelids drooped with need of sleep. But their hearts were light and their hearts were proud. They had a house of worship, where they and their children might gather together to sing the praises of God and to learn better how to follow His ways.

—Grace W. McGavran

The Fable of Heaven and Hell[11]

A popular fable tells the story of a good man who died and went to heaven. Upon approaching the Keeper of the Gates, he made a strange request to visit hell a few days before taking up his heavenly residence. Permission was granted, and he was amazed at what he found below. He saw huge banquet tables piled high with delectable foods fit for kings. But all the people were emaciated, lean, anemic. They were starving to death. Knives and forks, six feet long, were strapped to their hands and fingers so that they could never reach their mouths. Try as they did, they could not get one bite of food. The startled visitor had enough. He hurried back to heaven, and on entering there he saw practically the same scene: the same kind of banquet tables, the same kind of long knives and forks strapped to the hands and fingers of the people. But there was one big difference. The saints were pictures of health and strength and they came in to dinner laughing together. As the newcomer stood by breathlessly, they approached the tables and gathered generous helpings of food with their clinking silverware. Then heaven's happy host turned around and began feeding each other! This had never occurred to the people in hell. According to the fable, that's why they were down there in the first place.

—Frank Johnson Pippin

Where Love Is[12]

In a certain town there lived a shoemaker named Martin Avdeitch. He lived in a basement room which possessed but one window; the window looked out into the street, and through it could be caught a glimpse of the feet of the passers-by. Martin had always been an upright man, but with the approach of old age he had begun more than ever to think of his soul and draw nearer to God. . . .

His wife had died when he was still an apprentice, leaving behind her a little boy of three. Martin had been very happy with the little fellow for a while, but God had not seen fit to let his happiness with his child continue. Just as he was growing up and beginning to help his father the child fell ill and died after a few weeks of fever. Martin was inconsolable. Indeed he began to murmur against God; he wished only to die. "I am a lonely, hopeless man," he said to a peasant pilgrim who stopped one day at his place. The man objected to this attitude, saying, "You should not speak like that, Martin. It is not for us to judge the acts of God. We must rely, not upon our own understanding, but upon

Divine Wisdom. God saw fit that your son should die and that you should live. Therefore, it must be better so. If you despair it is because you have wished to live too much for your own pleasure."

"For what, then, should I live?" asked Martin.

"For God alone," replied the old man. "Christ has shown us the way. Can you read? If so, buy a New Testament and study it. You will learn there how to live for God."

Martin took these words to heart, and he began to read the New Testament. At first he was set to read only on festival days, but he found it so comforting that he never let a day pass without reading some. Gradually life began to change for him. He turned his back on the wasteful life he had been living since his little boy died. His life became quiet and joyous.

One night, while reading late, he came to the scene where the woman in the house of the rich Pharisee anointed Jesus' feet with her tears. And Jesus rebuked the Pharisee, saying, "Thou gavest me no water for my feet. . . . Thou gavest me no kiss . . . my head with oil thou didst not anoint." Martin took off his glasses and began to ponder, "I am even as that Pharisee. I drink tea and think only of my own needs. Yes, I think only of having plenty to eat and drink, of being warm and clean—but never of entertaining a guest. If the Lord should come to visit me, should I receive Him any better than Simon, the Pharisee?" Thinking thus, he fell asleep. Then someone spoke his name. "Who is there?" he asked; leaning forward and peering into the darkness he could see no one. Then the voice spoke again—"Martin, Martin! Look thou into the street tomorrow, for I am coming to visit thee."

The next morning Martin rose before daylight, sure that the voice he had heard in the night had been but a dream; yet somehow he could not put away the hope and the fear that it might have been the Christ. As Martin sat by the window that day he was almost ashamed that he kept looking up at the feet of those who passed by, as if expecting that Christ would really come. Not far into the morning, he recognized the feet of an old soldier, Stepanitch, who kept himself out of charity by helping a neighboring tradesman shovel snow. For a while Martin watched the feet of the old man in patched boots working wearily at the snow. Often he had to stop and rest. Suddenly Martin began to think: "He is evidently an old man now, and broken. He is not strong to clear away snow. Would he like some tea, I wonder?" With that he went out and implored Stepanitch to come in and have some warm refreshment. Stepanitch came in and rested for an hour with Martin, as they discussed the strange guest whom Martin was expecting that day. Stepanitch was an old man. Tears came easily to his eyes as Martin talked of the wonderful Christ who once walked with men. When he left he said, "I thank you, Martin Avdeitch. You have taken me in and fed both soul and body."

Some time later, Martin saw the feet of a poor, shabbily dressed woman stop in front of his window. Looking up he noticed that she was young and that she carried a baby in her arms; both were

87

trembling with the cold. Quickly Martin rushed out to them and besought the mother to come in with her child. As she sat near the stove warming herself she told Martin of her husband, who had been sent away as a soldier in the army eight months ago. "I had to pawn my last shawl yesterday for two coins." As she was leaving to go into the cold again, Martin rummaged about in a cupboard and finally came back to her with an old jacket. "Here, it is a poor old thing, but it will serve to cover you."

"I thank you, in Christ's name, good grandfather. Surely it was He Himself who sent me to your window. He, our Little Father, had placed you in your window, that you might see me in my bitter plight and have compassion on me."

The only other people Martin spoke with that day were an old woman and a little boy who was trying to steal the apples the poor old soul was carrying home. Martin rushed out into the street and stopped the theft. He reconciled the two—taking away the wrath of the woman in forgiveness, and shaming the boy into penitence. As the old woman was raising her sack of shavings to her shoulder to go on, the boy rushed forward and cried, "Nay, let me carry it, grandmother, it will be all on my way home."

Martin returned to his room. It was nearly dark now, and he put away his work, seating himself once more with his New Testament. He had intended reading where he left off last night but instead the book opened itself to another place. As he began to read he thought he heard a movement in the room. Then a voice whispered in his ear, "Martin, Martin, dost thou not know Me?"

"Who art thou?" said Martin.

"Even I," whispered the voice again. "Lo, it is I"—and Stepanitch appeared from the dark corner. He smiled and faded into the darkness.

"It is I," whispered the voice again—and there stepped from the same corner the woman and her baby.

"And it is I," whispered the voice again—and there came forth the old woman and the boy with the apples. Joy filled the soul of Martin Avdeitch. He put on his spectacles to read. At the top of the page were the words: "For I was an hungred, and ye gave me meat: I was thirsty, and ye gave me drink: I was a stranger, and ye took me in . . . Inasmuch as ye have done it unto one of the least of these my brethren, ye have done it unto me." Then Martin understood in truth that the Saviour had visited him and that he had received Him.

—Leo Tolstoy

Christian Stewardship

Purposes of a Stewardship Emphasis

In Alan Paton's poignant book, *Cry, the Beloved Country*, a story of comfort in desolation, we read these beautiful words which describe so well man's place amidst both the beauty and the desolation of the created world.

> There is a lovely road that runs from Ixopo into the hills. These hills are grass-covered and rolling, and they are lovely beyond any singing of it. . . .
>
> The grass is rich and matted, you cannot see the soil. It holds the rain and the mist, and they seep into the ground, feeding the streams in every kloof. It is well-tended, and not too many cattle feed upon it; not too many fires burn it, laying bare the soil. Stand unshod upon it, for the ground is holy, being even as it came from the Creator. Keep it, guard it, care for it, for it keeps men, guards men, cares for men. Destroy it and man is destroyed.
>
> Where you stand the grass is rich and matted, you cannot see the soil. But the rich green hills break down. They fall to the valley below, and falling, change their nature. For they grow red and bare; they cannot hold the rain and mist, and the streams are dry in the kloofs. Too many cattle feed upon the grass, and too many fires have burned it. Stand shod upon it, for it is coarse and sharp, and the stones cut under the feet. It is not kept, or guarded,

This chapter, through page 102, is from *Stewards in God's World* by John and Ruth Ensign, pp. 37-48, 92-93, 106. John Knox Press, 1953. (Slightly revised.)

or cared for, it no longer keeps men, guards men, cares for men. The titihoya does not cry here any more.

The great red hills stand desolate, and the earth has torn away like flesh. The lightning flashes over them, the clouds pour down upon them, the dead streams come to life, full of the red blood of the earth. Down in the valleys women scratch the soil that is left, and the maize hardly reaches the height of a man. They are valleys of old men and old women, of mothers and children. The men are away, the young men and the girls are away. The soil cannot keep them any more.[1]

This is not an isolated phenomenon of a portion of Africa. It is true across the face of the earth. Through careless land usage, great civilizations of the past in Northern China, Mesopotamia, Palestine, North Africa, and Peru have disappeared and their lands become desolate.

Even in the United States, long thought of as the land of plenty and opportunity, erosion, "the enemy of civilizations," has already destroyed or seriously impoverished 282,000,000 acres of American lands and impaired the productivity of 775,000,000 acres more. From our farm land alone the annual loss is about three billion tons of topsoil, enough to fill a freight train which would girdle the globe eighteen times. We are also using and wasting other natural resources faster than they can be restored. Fifty-four billion board feet of lumber are being cut in this country each year while the annual growth is only approximately thirty-five billion board feet. Thus during the last thirty-six years the nation's woodpile has been reduced forty-four per cent.

In his book, *Our Plundered Planet,* Fairfield Osborn makes a strong point of the danger that faces the world, and especially our American civilization; the fact that while our population is increasing rapidly, our natural resources to feed and maintain life are decreasing even more rapidly. He concludes:

> The question remains. Are we to continue on the same dusty perilous road once traveled to its dead end by other mighty and splendid nations, or, in our wisdom, are we going to choose the only route that does not lead to the disaster that has already befallen so many other peoples of the earth?[2]

As Christians we are doubly concerned about this problem. These resources that are being wasted are God-given gifts for man to care for and to use. Slowly we are realizing that to waste these resources not only hurts our own standard of living and jeopardizes our chance of survival, but it is actually a sin against the God who gave men dominion over the earth. Thus Christians are interested in conservation of

90

natural resources for religious reasons as well as for self-preservation, or for utilitarian concerns.

In planning a guide to bring Junior High boys and girls to an awareness of man's predicament in the face of this vast wastage of life and living things, our primary concern is that they come to the place where they see themselves as stewards of God—a stewardship that involves the whole of one's life. Christian stewardship is a way of life.

There are five specific purposes involved in an understanding of the whole matter of Christian stewardship. Briefly they are these:

1. To become increasingly aware of the natural resources God has provided for us in our world.
2. To become more aware of man's complete dependence upon God's provision of resources for his basic needs—food, clothing, shelter.
3. To come to a realization of God's plan for the world through the interdependence of all forms of life, the cycle of life and death, the place of evil in the realm of nature, and the natural interdependence of the world community of people.
4. To see what man has done to disrupt God's plan and what man must do as a steward of the land to conserve what is left.
5. To develop a deep sense of stewardship in relation to our natural resources, and to our bodies, our abilities, and our lives.

Ways of Achieving These Purposes Through Camp Activities

A. *To become increasingly aware of the natural resources God has provided for us in our world.*

Camp affords an ideal setting in which boys and girls can come to discover in a firsthand way the resources at our disposal, the soil, trees, plants, birds, animals, and water. Observing these things deepens an awareness and appreciation of the beauty and design, the variety, and the orderliness of nature as God has made it.

Every activity that takes campers around camp and the neighboring areas can make the campers more aware of our natural resources. It is fun to observe trees, plant life, birds and animals. Campers should learn to know the trees and wild plants and animals common to the woods. The number of different kinds will amaze them.

Meadows, fields, and prairies offer opportunities to observe grasses, plants, insects, small animals, birds, and flowers as you go. Take time to see them.

It is interesting to learn the story of time by observing the action of the elements on rock formations. Observe ways in which rocks are broken down to form soil.

Stoop down and examine the soil as you go. Is it rich in decayed matter? Or is it sandy or hard clay? Notice the topography of the land, its watersheds and ravines.

Boys and girls are intrigued by the life they find around water—lakes, ponds, marshes, and beaches. There's plenty of marine plant and animal life to see, birds to watch, and even soil to observe.

Special places near camp such as quarries, sawmills, farms, dairies, reforestation projects, and Indian territory offer unusual opportunities for becoming better acquainted with our natural resources.

An old stump can provide some interesting exploration by Junior Highs to determine age and rate of growth of the tree, rainfall, drought, and fire. One group of campers spent an hour of firsthand learning of conservation around an uprooted tree. Questions like, "What kind of tree is this?" and "What do you suppose caused this tree to fall over?" led to the seeking of many answers. The counselor insisted that evidence be found to verify each guess. Someone noted a rotten part in the center of the upturned stump and guessed its main taproot had rotted away. This was a good theory and caused much discussion about what happens when the only supporting roots are shallow ones. But this was not the main cause of the tree's falling, and the counselor pressed the group for a closer examination. One boy found one whole group of roots on one side of the stump that had been cut by an ax. The group noticed the clay markings of a refilled ditch nearby. Measurement proved that the roots had actually pulled up from this point. Further study showed that a water line had been laid in this ditch. The group concluded that more care should be taken in the locating of water lines in order to preserve the trees on the campsite. They had learned a real lesson in conservation that is a problem in any construction whether in camp or city.

B. *To become more aware of man's complete dependence upon God's provision of resources for his basic needs—food, clothing, shelter.*

The camp situation is ideal for providing opportunities to learn firsthand just how dependent we are upon nature for our basic needs—the materials for shelter, food, water; the materials for our clothing; the way in which weather exerts control over our activities. In our modern civilization we tend to get so far away from the source of these necessities that we begin to lose our sense of dependency upon God for providing them.

Shelter. The construction of a home-in-the-woods or small group campsite which includes the making of tables, benches, or shelters makes campers more dependent upon natural materials to meet their needs. It also involves the practice of the best conservation principles that good stewards can use so far as natural resources are concerned. In the first place, the location of the campsite must be determined with regard to drainage, density and size of trees, water supply, ground covering, and the effects of clearing. Will clearing a particular camp area cause future erosion? Can a sufficiently fireproof campfire area be cleared so that fire won't spread through roots to break out elsewhere?

The actual construction with wood involves a wise selection of saplings so that future supplies will not be depleted and that one area will not be hurt by taking too many. Boys and girls will have to learn the difference between trees and why certain kinds are used in preference to others. They will need to learn to use a simple tree key to tell the difference between a dogwood, which should not be cut in most states, and a hickory or oak or some other tree that may be plentiful in a particular area.

Food. Cook-outs raise the whole question of food—food supplies, balanced diet, methods of cooking, selection of firewood and the cutting and storage of it, proper place for a fire in relation to trees, ground fire hazards, and the use of natural foods that the area provides. The matter of garbage disposal raises the question of making a compost heap for the camp, which is a logical outcome of a good stewardship program.

Water. Any group working away from the main camp soon learns the importance of safe drinking water. This leads to an observation of the ways in which animals and plant life are also dependent upon water for their life. Then there is the matter of proper drainage around living areas so that refuse disposal and latrines do not pollute streams or drain into any source of water used for drinking.

Clothing. Some camps are in locations where the source of supplies for clothing manufacturing are found—cotton, flax, wool, furs. In one camp the campers visited a local farm on one of their hikes. Here they found a whole flock of sheep grazing on a hillside. The farmer had found that his slope was more productive kept in pasture for his sheep than if it had been cultivated for food. In some places a farmer or his wife could outline the process from raw product to finished material.

Weather. Campers, living in the out-of-doors, soon discover the importance of weather in their lives. Camping activities and plans depend to a great extent on what the weather is, and so the observation and prediction of weather becomes an important and useful activity. This may lead to the construction of a simple weather station.

Direction. On hikes through woods or across plains with no paved roads, perhaps no trails even, campers learn the value of a compass, or knowledge of the stars, the sun, and other outdoorsman ways of getting a sense of direction. Through such dependence upon the laws of the universe, campers learn how dependable God's laws are.

Campcraft. The whole realm of campcrafts affords opportunity to make conservation real to the Junior High campers. In an established camp careful selection becomes a matter of vital need, and conservation is the only answer to assuring future campers of a source of materials. One camper, sensing this, said, "Why, if we aren't careful our children won't have sassafras with which to make baskets." Crafts in camp ought to use native materials, but this means careful selection to insure a supply for future campers. Many vines, fibers, and cattails can be used with little fear of depleting the native resources; whereas splints (from sassafras, white oak, hickory) for baskets, and tree bark for lashing, must be chosen with great care. Much use can be made of the bark of fallen trees, and dead cedar and fruit tree wood are good sources for carving wood. Native clay can often be used for pottery work, but care must be taken to avoid erosion caused by stripping an area of topsoil or ground cover in order to get the clay.

All of these activities will provide excellent learning opportunities to help Junior High campers become increasingly aware of the natural resources God has given to man, and of man's dependence upon these for his basic needs. The counselor's task is to take the inherent interest in wildlife, trees, and native crafts, and help the campers interpret their experiences in such a way that they will grow in their sense of dependence upon the God who created these things.

C. *To come to a realization of God's plan for our world through:*

1. *The interdependence of all living things and the balance which must be maintained between them if life is to continue*

Campers are usually thrilled when they learn how people breathe in oxygen and breathe out carbon dioxide which is turned back into oxygen by plants which absorb the carbon dioxide and "breathe out" oxygen. When one boy in camp discovered that a similar exchange goes on between plant and animal life in the water, he excitedly exclaimed, "Isn't God just wonderful!"

The interdependence of plants, insects, and animals is truly marvelous: the bee that fertilizes the flower as it gathers nectar; the birds that scatter the seeds of plants; the squirrels that often plant seeds by failing to gather all they've buried; and the earthworms and ants that cultivate the soil around plants.

94

Serious trouble occurs when the balance in nature is broken. For years deer have been protected by closed seasons on hunting, and now in many places they are so numerous that they have been forced to seek food beyond their former woodlands and have become pests to adjacent farmlands.

Men have also upset nature's balance by killing for sport too many of certain species of birds and animals. In some cases entire species have been destroyed.

Nature's cycle is again broken with far-reaching effects on both plant and animal life when land is plowed that should be kept in grass or woodland and is thus exposed to erosion.

2. *The interpretation of the cycle of life and death and new life again, and the natural laws governing this process*

Boys and girls are often puzzled and frightened by death and welcome any chance to help solve the mystery it holds for them. One city woman who moved to the country was amazed to discover that putting the dead plants from one season's flowers on her flower bed produced better plants the next year. This led her to an evaluation of the part death plays in the whole cycle of life. She concluded, "If something so simple seeming as a leaf does not really die, then the orderliness or pattern of the earth would not logically permit something as complex and important as the human soul to go into utter nothingness at death."[3]

It helps campers to see the effects of decayed trees, plants, and animals on the fertility of the soil. Making a camp compost heap—which is real conservation—is a practical demonstration of this cycle and shows the effects of the bacteria which cause dead plants and animals to decay.

3. *The place of evil in the realm of nature*

Many questions come to the campers' minds about why God made things that seem evil—poison ivy and poison sumac, poisonous snakes and insects which are harmful to men, and unexplainable disasters like earthquakes and tornadoes, lightning and floods, which destroy life and property. It is well to admit man's inability to explain the "why" of some of these evils, and like Job to cease from questioning the wisdom of what seem to be some of God's ways. Jesus went beyond the questioning of "why" a particular man was born blind to the potentiality for good that lay dormant there. Then He proceeded to heal the man.

Men for centuries lived in fear of the lightning. Today men have succeeded in controlling the path of lightning to a great extent in the places where people live. Even more important, men have learned to harness some of the vast electrical energy in our world and have given us the benefits of electricity.

Some day, perhaps, men will learn to harness and use for good some of the other things which seem evil in our world. Doctors have recently seen hope in the use of rattlesnake venom as a possible aid in curing some of our dread diseases. Maybe even the poisonous snakes have their potential for good!

Men are learning to control some of the poisonous plants, too, although sometimes such harmful things serve to make us a bit more careful and more humble in the way we handle the things of nature.

4. *The natural interdependence of the world community*

Global trade in food and products forms the largest industry in the world. Our tastes have become world wide, and even in camp we use foods from many lands. Men today are realizing more than ever before the importance of the question, "Am I my brother's keeper?" When one part of the world impoverishes its resources, the rest of the world suffers too. Plowing grasslands in the Midwest started dust storms there that blew halfway across the continent. Hunger in one part of the world brings helpless refugees to another part. Depleted lands give rise to hunger and revolution, and revolution soon affects the world. Christian stewards cannot help but take to heart Jesus' words concerning the hungry and the sick: "As you did it to one of the least of these my brethren, you did it to me."

D. *To see what man has done to disrupt God's plan and what man must do as a steward of the land to conserve what is left.*

Exploration trips around camp and the surrounding countryside will offer a wealth of opportunity to observe firsthand some of the ways in which men have wasted and misused natural resources. These observations may come as a by-product of a berry-picking trip, walks from the main camp to the "home-in-the-woods," or an all-camp trip to a special spot outside camp. This was true of one camp's visit to a lovely picnic spot. On the way they passed through a devastated forest and poorly kept farm to another farm where good conservation practices were everywhere in evidence.

1. *Observation of what man has done to deplete our resources*

Notice evidences of erosion by water or wind. Look for it along trails, in ravines, on hillsides, and near the lake or other body of water.

Walks along roadcuts show areas of topsoil and subsoil and often show effects of erosion.

Check depth of topsoil in cultivated and uncultivated fields, in grassed and ungrassed fields, and in forest and open field.

Rainy days are excellent for observation of erosion. Put on rain clothes and go out. See where the rain runs off—the gullies it forms and the amount of soil it carries with it. Catch water samples. Put marked stakes at the head of a gully before a rain and check afterward to see the amount of soil that washed away.

Stump exploration gives clues to years of drought, to fire, to amounts of rainfall, to times of good and poor growth, and to age of trees.

Observe the logging practices that have taken place in woodlands. Were they good or bad? Have trees been left lying on the ground? Did falling trees hurt other trees as they fell? Have tops been left, creating a real fire hazard?

Notice any burned-over areas to see the effect on plant and animal life. Are there evidences of past fires on trees in areas that now show little signs of fire?

See if there is any water pollution of streams, lakes, or swimming area.

Take trips to abandoned farm land to observe nature taking over in the process of reclamation.

Check with local farmers to learn about the abundance of game and fish as compared to a generation or so ago.

Check on rare plants and why they are so rare.

Observe tree and plant parasites. Find reasons why they are so prevalent.

See if any animals such as deer are overprotected for the amount of food available for them. Do any farmers keep herds of cattle that are too large for the available pasturage?

See the effects of "open range" for cattle on woodland in which they roam. Notice effects of their hoofs on tree roots. Have the cattle destroyed lower tree limbs? Look for similar effects in wooded areas that people use constantly. Does packing down the soil around trees hurt them? Why?

Observe stunted growth due to depleted soil. Investigate ways of improving it.

Notice tree diseases that have taken hold where bulldozers scraped them, or where the trees were injured by blazing marks or other cuts. Observe places where tree injuries have healed.

Notice ways in which trees compensate for hindrances to their growth—the way trees bend and grow around things in their way.

Observe neighboring farms. Have areas been cultivated with row crops that would better have been left in grass or woodland? Have crops been planted up and down a slope so that rain water washes off too fast?

2. *Conservation activities that campers can carry on in camp*

Make check dams in ravines and gullies where rain water runs off too fast.

Make diversion ditches on hillside trails to divert the run-off water to areas of growth where it can be better absorbed by the soil.

With the aid of county agricultural agent secure seedlings for reforestation projects. The county agent will also aid in securing plants for bird food and cover for planting on edges of woodlands, in gullies, on banks, and in abandoned roads. Ravines, otherwise useless, make perfect bird sanctuaries when planted with the right cover plants. These plants vary with the locality.

Seeding projects, like quick-growing grass or cover crops, in areas that need planting.

Terrace slopes to prevent erosion.

Transplant plants from overcrowded areas to depleted areas. Do minor tree surgery where it is needed on injured trees. (Major tree surgery requires the help of an expert or trained person.)

Use selective cutting of saplings for campcraft projects.

Erosion-control projects wherever needed—along trails and roadsides, near shelter areas, and on lake or stream banks. Use rocks and staked logs until proper plantings take hold.

Correct pollution from camp drainage system if needed.

Make a habit of proper fire building—careful selection of place to make a fire and of type to be used. Know how to clear area to keep fire from spreading.

See that all fires are extinguished so that there is no chance of the fire's going underground or flaring up later. Make firebreaks for fire control in forests and on prairies. Let these cutbacks double as trails.

Maintain and use trails to prevent erosion and to keep destruction of plant life at a minimum.

Encourage selectivity in the collection of samples of flowers, plants, and wild animals. Gather according to abundance. Know which plants are protected by state law, which plants must be picked sparingly, and which can be gathered in quantity.

Know and avoid contact with noxious plants. Seek ways to control these plants in the camp area.

Learn ways to control or to wipe out tree and plant parasites, pests, and diseases—the caterpillar, rust, etc.

Control rodent and insect pests. Use rodent-tight food boxes. Leave harmless snakes that feed on rodents.

Build and maintain a compost pile. Use food scraps, leaves, and dead plants.

Encourage selectivity in gathering materials for crafts and table decorations.

Discourage overraking around shelter areas and campsites. This destroys natural undergrowth, can lead to erosion and loss of moisture around roots, and causes excessive dust. Select a good place for playing games so that plants, grass, and bushes will not be excessively injured. Perhaps rotate such play areas.

Preserve and care for useful camp items like cooking sticks, clay, and lashed benches and tables so that there will be as little need as possible to take supplies and make new ones.

The idea of one group of campers bequeathing these things to following group is a good one and encourages such conservation.

Encourage proper use of campsite—lashing instead of nailing, location of site with a consideration of privacy and beauty, and use of proper sanitation and refuse disposal.

Mark trails with rocks or stakes. Do not use blazes.

In gathering berries and other natural foods, take care to leave some for birds. There is an absence of edible plants like berries, fruits, and nuts where good conservation practices are not followed.

Secure aid of agricultural agent or Conservation Department to advise on the use and development of camp streams and waters.

Know state regulations for fishing and observe them

E. *To develop a sense of stewardship in relation to our natural resources, and to our bodies, our abilities, and our lives.*

1. *Stewardship of natural resources*

There is a difference between conservation and stewardship of our natural resources. Conservation is the preservation and wise use of these resources. Stewardship goes deeper than that—it is conservation motivated by a realization and acknowledgment of God as the giver and sustainer of all these things as well as of human life itself.

> "All that we have is Thine alone,
> A trust, O Lord, from Thee."

In a camp that is seeking to develop Christian stewardship, this distinction is most important. Without it camping becomes more of a secular experience: with this motivation camping can become a religious experience.

2. *Stewardship of our bodies*

A faithful steward thinks of his body as "a temple of God," and keeps it as healthy as possible because it is God-given. Junior Highs are naturally interested in their bodies because of the rapid changes taking place in them. They are desirous of making themselves the best they can be physically, in appearance, and in strength. Girls of this age spend hours combing their hair, and boys go to great lengths in trying to develop physical prowess.

Camp is an ideal place for boys and girls to gain some practical experience in healthy ways of living. Doing it together in a group is more fun. Filling their own schedule with exciting activities means that enough hours must be allotted to sleep, so that they will be sufficiently rested to enjoy their program. Meal planning for cook-outs brings before them the need of balancing their diets. Failure to care for our bodies limits our capacity to be faithful stewards in the other areas of life.

3. Stewardship of our abilities and our lives

God gives each of us certain abilities. Many of these are common to all people, like the capacity to love and be loved. Some abilities are more rare and we think of people with these talents as being gifted in their special ways—the artist, musician, or preacher. Jesus' story of the Talents describes most effectively the whole matter of the stewardship of our abilities and our lives. (See Matthew 25.) Jesus shows us that God, by giving us life itself, offers us the opportunity of being good stewards of our abilities—common or rare. When we use them faithfully they increase. This is as true of the capacity to love as it is of the talent of an artist. When we fail to use an ability or talent we lose it. Even our Christian faith is not ours until we make use of it and share it.

This parable of the Talents brings home to the campers in a very real way the meaning of stewardship. In their small groups the campers learn to use their abilities for the good of the group. A wise and sympathetic counselor can help the boys and girls go beyond the group application and apply this parable to their own lives. Such personal application can lead to decisions that are vital and meaningful to the Junior Highs.

Helpful Scripture Passages

1. The Natural Resources God Has Provided in Our World

Genesis 1 and 2—The creation story.
Psalm 104—A song of creation.
Psalm 8—Man's place in God's world.
Psalm 19:1-6—The heavens tell of God's glory.
Psalm 24:1-2—The earth is the Lord's.
Psalm 33:1-9—The heavens were made.

100

Psalms of praise for the world—Select passages from Psalms 92, 93, 95, 96, 97, 98, and all of 100 and 148.

Psalm 65:9-13—The blessing of rain.

2. Man's Dependence upon God for His Basic Needs

Dependence Upon God

Genesis 1:26-31—Interdependence of plants, animals, and man.
Genesis 8:22—Dependability.
Psalm 23—The Shepherd Psalm.
Psalm 36:5-10—The steadfastness of God's love.
Psalm 65:9-13—Abundance of the harvest.
Psalm 104—The plan of the world.
Psalm 111:5—God provides food.
Psalm 147:7-9 and 14-18—He gives food.
Proverbs 6:6-11—Ants provide their food.
Proverbs 30:24-28—The wisdom of small things of the earth.
Song of Solomon 2:11-13a—The winter is past, the flowers appear.
Isaiah 40:28—God is never weary.
Isaiah 41:18-20—God provides rivers and trees.
Isaiah 44:14-16—Gift of fire.
Isaiah 55—God offers good things to all.
Matthew 6:25-33—God's care.
Mark 4:26-29—Seedtime and harvest.

Being Unafraid

Psalm 27—Confidence in God.
Psalm 121—God's care for the traveler.

3. God's Plan for the World

Plan for Interdependence of Life

Genesis 1:26-31—Interdependence of plants, animals, and man.
Psalm 104—The plan of the world.
Job 33:12 and 13—Job questions evil in the world. (See passages from chapters 38 and 39 and Job's final answer in 42:1-6.)

Cycle of Life and Death

Psalm 90:1-12—The frailty of human life.
Psalm 104:27-30—Life-giving power of God.
John 12:24—Sacrifice of life brings a harvest.
I Corinthians 15:35-44—Paul compares the death of a seed and the death of man.

4. Faithful Stewardship of the Land

Genesis 2:15—Man to keep the garden.
Leviticus 26:3-6, 14-20, 33—God's promise to those who keep His commandments and warning to those who do not.
Deuteronomy 8:1-20—How to live in God's good land.
Jeremiah 12:10-11—Man's unconcern for the land.
Jeremiah 2:7—Men fail God.
Joel 2:3b—A garden before man and a wilderness after him.

5. Faithful Stewardship in All of Life

Faithful Stewardship of Our Bodies

I Corinthians 3:16-17—You are a temple of the Holy Spirit.
Matthew 10:28-31—You are of more value than many sparrows.
Luke 12:22-31—Be not anxious about your body.
Luke 2:52—Jesus increased in wisdom and in stature . . .

Faithful Stewardship of Our Lives

Matthew 25:14-30—The talents.
Matthew 4:18-22 and 9:9—Calling of the disciples.
Matthew 10:8b—Give as it has been given to you.
Matthew 13:3-9, 18-23—The sower.
Matthew 13:31-32—The mustard seed.
Matthew 19:16-22—The rich young ruler—Go, give, come . . .
Matthew 25:31-46—Caring for the hungry and thirsty, the strangers, etc.
John 15:1-11—The vine and the branches.
John 15:12-17—Friendship with Jesus.
John 3:16—Everlasting life.
I Corinthians 12:4-31—The varieties of service but all one body in Christ.
II Corinthians 9:6-15—The blessing of giving.
Philippians 4:8—Think of these things.

Hymns Particularly Appropriate for Christian Stewardship Emphasis

For the Beauty of the Earth
God Who Touchest Earth with Beauty
All Creatures of Our God and King
This Is My Father's World
That Cause Can Neither Be Lost nor Stayed
Fairest Lord Jesus
Praise Ye the Lord, the Almighty, the King of Creation
God of the Earth, the Sky, the Sea
Beauty Around Us
Day Is Dying in the West
Praise the Lord: Ye Heavens, Adore Him
Joyful, Joyful, We Adore Thee
Open Mine Eyes, That I May See
Take My Life, and Let It Be
Just As I Am, Thine Own to Be
Take Thou Our Minds, Dear Lord
All Praise to Thee, My God, This Night (Stanza 1 only)
God, That Madest Earth and Heaven (Stanza 1 only)
Now on Land and Sea Descending (Stanzas 1, 2, and 4)
We Give Thee But Thine Own
We Plow the Fields
O Worship the King

Resources in Prose and Poetry

An Eleventh Commandment

In 1939, Dr. Walter C. Lowdermilk, Associate Chief of the Soil Conservation Service, was sent by the United States government to the Near East to learn why the flourishing civilizations of Bible times had ceased to exist. During his extensive study of this barren area he found ruined cities buried under the products of soil erosion, dried-up stream beds, ancient irrigation systems, and remnants of once forested areas. His conclusion was that man's failure to be a good steward of God's gifts to mankind was the direct cause of the desolation around him.

Before leaving Jerusalem, Dr. Lowdermilk was invited to speak on the radio, and in planning what he would say, he found himself wondering if in the time of Moses there could not have been added an 11th commandment in the light of the calamity that was to befall the land. Putting his thoughts on paper, he later broadcast what has now become known as an "Eleventh Commandment."

"Thou shalt inherit the Holy Earth as a faithful steward, conserving its resources and productivity from generation to generation. Thou shalt safeguard thy fields from soil erosion, thy living waters from drying up, thy forests from desolation, and protect thy hills from overgrazing by thy herds, that thy descendants may have abundance forever. If any shall fail in this stewardship of the land, thy fruitful fields shall become sterile, stony ground and wasting gullies, and thy descendants shall decrease and live in poverty or perish from off the face of the earth."[1]

Stewardship

O Lord of heaven and earth and sea,
To Thee all praise and glory be!
How shall we show our love to Thee,
    Who givest all?
The golden sunshine, vernal air,
Sweet flowers and fruit Thy love declare;
When harvests ripen, Thou art there,
    Who givest all.
To Thee, from whom we all derive
Our life, our gifts, our power to give:
Oh, may we ever with Thee live,
    Who givest all!

—Christopher Wordsworth (1807-1885)

Going to School to God[2]

I like to go to school to God!
    I hear such strange, revealing things;
He talks to me where rivers run
    And where a skylark soars and sings.

He teaches me His love and care
    Through every tree and blade of grass
Here on the hill, where I may sit
    And listen while the wild winds pass.

He writes with glaciers on the rocks
    And with the stars that blaze on high;
With fossil shells and ferns that fall
    And leave their imprint when they die.

His books are beds of slate and coal;
    His manuscripts sequoia trees;
While earthquakes punctuate the tale
    And turn the pages of the seas.

His blackboard is a canyon wall
    Whereon he writes of ages past.
In even lines the strata tell
    Of things that shall forever last.

He writes with rivers, and they carve
    The crevices He leaves, to tell
The story of His living love
    In temple, tower, and pinnacle.

I like to go to school to God
    Because it always seems to me
He talks in every breeze that blows;
    Through every bud, and bird, and bee.
             —William L. Stidger

STORIES

The Clocks Stood Still[3]

"Just one more story, Grandpa," begged George and Jean. A lighthouse keeper who was once a sea captain makes the best kind of a story-telling grandfather. The howling of the wind outside made the fire of driftwood in the lighthouse living room all the more snug.

"I'm afraid it's bedtime for two children who are taking the train back to the city tomorrow morning." Grandfather pulled his big gold watch from his pocket, looked at it, and gave a little snort of disgust. "Well, of all the absent-minded old sea captains! Now that we have electric clocks in almost every room, I forget to wind my watch. With you catching the train tomorrow, we might as well have the correct time anyway."

Grandfather walked across the room. He did not even glance at the electric clock on the desk, but turned on the radio. An orchestra was just bringing its concerts to a close. They waited while a voice urged them to buy something, and then listened for the time announcement. It came, "The correct time is now exactly—"

A whir. Then silence—and darkness.

"Wh-wh-what—" the children began. But the old lighthouse keeper did not bother with questions. If the current was off in the living room, the lights were out in the great dome above. There was a heavy wind at sea, and ships were depending on that light. Grandfather felt his way to the kitchen, lighted a lantern and was halfway to the tower stairs before George and Jean had caught their breath.

The children trailed after the sputtering lantern and reached the top of the long spiral staircase in time to see their grandfather light the enormous kerosene lamp which was always kept clean and filled, ready for just such an emergency. It took some time to get the old lamp adjusted so that its glow was so strong and steady that the lighthouse keeper would trust it to burn through the night. There was something so quaint and mellow about its glow that George and Jean wanted to stay up there beside it and ply their grandfather with questions about the time, before they were born, when that lamp had burned every night.

"Come, come," said Grandfather finally. "It was bedtime when all this began. It is nobody-knows-how-long after bedtime now."

When they reached the living quarters again, the darkness had been driven away by the kerosene lamps which Grandmother had lighted while they were busy with the big lamp in the dome. Grandfather took out his old gold watch again, wound it, and looked at the electric clock on the desk. The children looked too. The clock, of course, was just as dead as the radio or the electric lights.

"How shall we ever know when it is train time tomorrow?" asked George.

Jean rushed to the wall telephone and rang the signal vigorously. There was no response.

"The same wind that fixed our electric lights must have finished our telephone wires," said Grandmother.

"No neighbors and no telephone," said Jean.

"No radio and no clock," finished George.

The children looked at their grandfather, expecting him to be just as lost as they. There was a merry twinkle in his eye.

"You poor little landlubbers!" The old lighthouse keeper burst into a hearty laugh. "You haven't much faith in your old seafaring grandfather." More quietly he added, "Nor much faith in the God who set the lights of the heavens in their courses."

"God gave us electricity," said George solemnly, "but it isn't doing us much good right now."

"God did give us electricity, but it comes to us through man-made instruments that may go wrong," said Grandfather. "When God set the lights of heaven in their appointed courses, he put them so far away that man has not interfered with them."

Jean and George looked at Grandfather hopefully.

"Many's the time in my seafaring days that I set my watch with nothing but the stars and this little instrument to guide me." Grandfather had taken the shining brass sextant from its place on the shelf and was stroking it as though he loved it. The children remembered the night last summer when they had stood on a rock near the sea while their grandfather pointed the sextant at the stars, measured their distances from the meridian, and figured the time of night correctly.

"Are we going to find the time with the sextant?" asked George, eager to be at it.

"That would take quite a while. There happens to be a much easier way that we can use tonight."

Grandfather took the paper-covered almanac from the table and tossed it into George's lap. "You see, the old moon goes so faithfully in the path the good Lord set for it that men who have studied the heavens are able to tell years ahead just when the moon will rise and set each day."

"The moon rose right after we went to bed last night," said Jean. "It will rise almost an hour later tonight. That might be soon. Quick, George! Find the page."

Jean ran to the window which gave a full view of the eastern horizon, as George thumbed through the almanac. Finding the page that told of the rising and setting of the moon in June of that year, he ran his finger down the column and found the date, June fifteenth.

"The moon is three days past full, and it rises today at twenty-four minutes past nine," reported George.

Grandfather nodded. "You watch there at the east window, Jean. While we are waiting, let's think of other ways we could set our clocks."

"We might set them by the time the sun rises tomorrow morning." George looked at the time of the sunrise on June sixteenth and added with a grin, "If we happen to be awake at twenty-two minutes past four tomorrow morning."

The lighthouse keeper beamed. "We may be able to make seamen out of you landlubbers after all. Now tell me another way that we could tell the time, not exactly, but very nearly."

Jean, looking out of the east window, watched the waves creeping higher and higher on the beach. Clapping her hands, she whirled about, crying, "By the tides, Grandpa, by the tides! The tide is nearly high now. Look in the almanac, George, and see when it is high this evening."

Quickly, George found the well-worn page in the almanac which helped them plan their daily swiming time. "High tide on June fifteenth at 9:56 P.M. That's just about half an hour after the moon rises. We can set our clocks when the moon rises at 9:24

and then see if the water covers the top of the sharp gray rock at 9:56."

"There's a silver light in the east," announced Jean from her lookout at the window.

Grandfather handed his watch to George, who joined Jean at the window. Silently they watched the sheen in the east grow brighter. They saw a point of golden light slowly grow into a half circle of glistening gold. George set the hands of the watch at 9:24 as the half circle of gold grew into a full globe. George pushed back the stem of the watch, and handed it back, ticking faithfully.

Good-nights said, and the old alarm clock wound and set, the children started on their belated trip to bed. Just as they were leaving the room carrying a lamp, the electric lights flared on and the voice from the radio resumed its interrupted chant. "You are listening to station WLDK. The correct time comes to you from the marine observatory. It is exactly twenty-nine minutes and eighteen seconds after nine o'clock, eastern standard time."

"Faithful old moon," said Jean, looking at the clock which agreed exactly with the time just heard.

George was slowly repeating something he had heard many times but had never really noticed before. "Marine—observatory—time. Observatory. Why, that's the place where they have telescopes and things to look at the stars and the planets. So they get the correct radio time from the skies, too."

"Of course," chuckled the old friend of the stars, the lighthouse keeper. "Men make mighty fine instruments, but they cannot quite trust them. When they want to be really sure of the passage of time, they ask the sun, the moon, the stars, and the planets which are still moving just as God taught them to move, millions of years ago."

—Alice Geer Kelsey

Nature's Engineers

It was one of those lovely evenings when the warm summer air hung close to the earth and a stillness lay over everything. Even the water hardly rippled against the shore. A small group of boys and their leader rested against the trees under which they had pitched their tents. Supper was over, their dishes done. They too were quiet watching the darkness steal over the land. It was good to be quiet after their long day's hike and the effort they had made to set up camp before darkness descended on them. They watched the twilight colors disappear from the sky and the first of the evening stars appear.

"Never knew it could be so quiet any place," said Don as he stretched out.

"Not a soul for miles around. It ought to be quiet," and Jim chuckled as he thought of how far they had come. "Didn't see a soul all day except you guys."

Several of the boys started to get ready to slip into their sleeping bags when Steve happened to notice something out in the water. It looked like someone swimming, but whatever it was was a mighty good swimmer because it didn't ruffle the surface of the water much and it appeared to be making good time. Steve looked puzzled.

"What's that out there?" The other boys strained their eyes too, and suddenly Don said, "I'll bet it's a beaver. Remember, when we were gathering firewood tonight we saw some trees that had been chewed a lot around the bottom of their trunks?"

"Yep," added Steve. "I bet you're right. But somebody ought to get rid of those beavers, the way they destroy trees. Those two big trees we saw took some time to grow that large and it's a shame to have them killed that way."

George, who had been whittling on a piece of wood, looked up at Steve. "You don't know much about beavers, do you?"

"Guess not," said Steve. "Why?"

"Oh, because, if you did, you wouldn't want to get rid of them. They're the smartest little animals, and they're the best conservationists God put in the woods."

"That's a laugh—the way they chewed up those trees we saw!" Bill moved into the group. "What do they conserve, dead trees?"

George smiled good-naturedly and looked at Irv, their leader. "Why don't we see if we can find the dam the beavers have probably made on this lake?"

"O.K. by me. I think it's a fine idea," said Irv. Quickly the boys gathered up their flashlights and started out along the edge of the lake.

"Looks as if there's good fishing in there, fellows. We'll have to try to catch a few in the morning." Irv loved to fish and his boys knew he'd be up early to try his luck.

"Say, what's this doing here?" Jim had come upon a rough mound of dirt and sticks not far from the edge of the water. He looked it over carefully. "Not a hole or a sign of life about it. How'd it get here? Nobody'd dump a pile of dirt and sticks way up here."

George caught Irv's eye and grinned. Irv asked, "But somebody or something put it there. It's pretty solid, isn't it?"

The boys pushed and poked at it a bit and found it was pretty solid.

"Oh, I bet it's a beaver's house," Steve beamed. "But there's no hole for a beaver to go in or out."

"Of course not," said George. "I told you they were smart. Their homes open under water so their enemies can't get them. They run tunnels underground from their homes into the lake. That house is made of sticks they've chewed. See, the bark's been eaten off. They chew the trees and branches into lengths they can handle. They pack mud around the sticks they use to make their house, to hold it all together. Look, here are some teeth marks. They have four big front teeth, two up and two down, that are as sharp as chisels."

The boys gathered around and talked about how a little 35-

pound animal could manage to cut down whole trees and get the logs and the sticks where they wanted them. As the boys looked farther around them they found a little channel dug in the ground running from the lake into the woods. Irv suggested that the next day they follow the channel back into the woods to see where the beavers had cut some trees and floated the pieces to the lake.

By this time Don had found the dam and the boys became engrossed in studying it. Some of the sticks in it were really logs and it all was very solidly constructed. It even had a curve in it facing upstream. Irv asked the boys to figure out why the beavers had curved it since a straight one would have been simpler to make.

Dave figured it out. "It'll withstand more water pressure, having a curve like that. It's a pretty good little stream comes in up at the end where we pitched our tents. But they do make them straight across sometimes. I've seen them. And I've seen some real long beaver dams too—several hundred feet long. The beavers kept adding to the one real long one I saw and they backed up a big lake there. Honest, you'd hardly believe it. They're real engineers."

On their way back to their camp they found more beaver homes. It was exciting to think how the beavers had changed this whole area that had once been only woods and a little mountain stream. Now there was a lake, holding back the stream's water, catching the debris and silt that flowed into it, providing a good place for shallow water plants and grasses to grow, and in which fish and other marine life could multiply. When the area got too crowded with beavers some would go off to a new site and start all over. And in time, the lake might fill up completely with silt, debris, and organic remains, and become a grassy meadow. Irv added that he'd read somewhere that perhaps one tenth of all the flat meadow land in the Rocky Mountain area had been created by beaver engineers.

As the boys slipped into their sleeping bags to settle down for the night, Steve chuckled, "Boy, we're lazy now compared to all those busy beavers out there. They're some builders. Somebody ought to give them their engineering degrees."

Jim added, "Well, with all the limitations on hunting them, I guess they're pretty well respected in spite of no degrees."

How Much Land Does a Man Need?[4]

There once was a Russian peasant who was very unhappy living in the city near all his relatives, and especially living near his in-laws. He became restless and dissatisfied and pretty soon he bartered his parcel of land for another. He was so successful in this deal that he decided to barter and sell more land. It wasn't long before he had attained quite a measure of wealth and he might have been very happy settling down on his new land in comfort.

However, the fever of acquiring land had gotten the better of him and he couldn't settle down. He was constantly on the lookout for new land, searching here and there and working out "good

109

deals." One day he found the lord of a neighboring province who was willing to make him a fabulous offer—1,000 rubles for as much land as the peasant could pace off in a day's time, from the place where the lord dropped his hat.

The peasant looked out over all the land that could become his—as far as he could see. When the lord dropped his hat the peasant started out full of high anticipation. He would really pace off a wonderful piece of land for himself! His eyes and his greed carried him far out over the land. The day wore on and as the shadows began to lengthen the peasant realized he had a very long distance to go to get back before dark to the place where the hat had been dropped. He began to quicken his pace and as the shadows lengthened far across the fields he started to run. Far ahead he could just barely see the place where the lord was waiting for him. As the sun began to slip behind the trees the peasant ran frantically, and finally amid cheers from the bystanders he fell to the ground and touched the hat at the feet of the lord. "You have done well. The land is yours," said the lord. But the man didn't move—he was dead. All he needed was six feet of ground—no more—in which to be buried.

—Leo Tolstoy

A Wound in the Earth

Early one summer morning a group of campers and their counselors slipped their packs on their backs and set out to climb a mountain. It took them all day to climb the rugged mountain trails to the top, but they arrived in time to view the surrounding valleys and mountains in the glow of the late afternoon sun. There, stretched before them, lay mile after mile of green mountain slopes, gloriously beautiful in the light of the setting sun.

But then, as the group turned around and looked in the opposite direction they gasped at what they saw. Out beyond the mountain they were on lay what looked like an ugly red wound on the earth. In the rays of the sunset it looked blood red, a terrifying contrast to the green of the surrounding mountains. It covered miles and miles of land.

What they were looking at was Copper Hill, Tennessee. Here years ago, men carelessly mined and processed the copper found in the earth. They allowed the fumes given off from their processing plants to go into the air where they combined with the elements of the air to make sulphuric acid which in time killed all the vegetation over a hundred-square-mile area in the mountains. When the plants and trees died they couldn't hold the soil on the slopes, and the rains washed the soil away leaving absolutely barren hillsides of red earth full of gullies fifteen and twenty feet deep. There wasn't a tree in sight—nor a blade of grass, for that matter.

Today men are trying to reclaim the land by setting out pine seedlings, or planting grass and kudzu vines. It's a hard task, for the plants have meagre nourishment in such barren soil. And

110

until their roots grow firm enough to hold the soil every rain threatens to wash them away too.

God's wealth of copper is still in those hills, but the land above it cannot support the life of men until men through costly effort replace the productivity of the soil. Men cannot be selfish and careless in their use of God's gifts without suffering the consequences.

To those campers standing on that mountaintop, the blood-red wound in the earth was an offense against God. In one direction the earth stretched out in all its beauty and grandeur as it came from the hand of God: in the other direction lay ugliness, waste, and desolation as a result of the hand of man.

Christian Growth

Purposes of a Christian Growth Emphasis

"**G**ROWING" is perhaps the most descriptive word that can be applied to Junior High boys and girls. They are growing every which way, from a self-conscious attitude toward their awkwardly developing bodies, through the ups and downs of social growth away from their parents in a group or gang where they find their new security, to the dawning realization of the vast challenge the world holds for them. It is at this age, when they are beginning to discover themselves as persons, that problems of life and faith really begin to confront them. In any group of Junior Highs there are great differences in development, and this is as true of mental and spiritual growth as it is of the more apparent physical development. Growth is not an even process; it has its spurts as well as its periods of slower stabilizing growth. Much depends on what nourishes it and the direction in which growth is taking place.

Christian growth is in many ways an intangible thing. We cannot say, "Go to now and grow in Christlikeness." We can see such growth when it has taken place, we can guide and encourage it, but we cannot specifically determine it. At best we can seek to provide situations which are as favorable to good growth as we can make them. Small group camping abounds in such opportunities when real group fellowship in the Body of Christ is developed with the guidance of mature and concerned Christian leaders who have come to understand their campers and their needs through the close daily living in camp.

We need to go to the very foundations of our faith if we are to have any idea of where we are going and why, in our effort to facilitate Christian growth in our campers. "Our starting point with them is the fact that they belong to God, that God is their Father, and that He is at work in their lives long before they can consciously understand anything of His purposes."[1] He is at work in them now and we may be a part of His purpose in their lives. We can help sow some seeds of spiritual growth but it is God working within them who provides the increase. We can help cultivate those awarenesses of God and of His purposes that are stirring within them and we may also be able to help harvest some of their growing understandings and perceptions. There come moments in which a growing life is ready to move forward in faith and may need help to achieve that growth. But we must also realize that God is personal in His encounter with a person and no one else can seek to control or mold the response of another—even in what he thinks are the "right" ways—without being a stumbling block to that other person.

> God is not willing to compel faith or obedience in any man. They have no value for him unless they are the free expression of a man's own being. . . . The Church has, far too often in the past, disowned this principle, being more anxious that men should conform to Christian standards of faith and conduct than that they should find their way to an immediate personal knowledge of God in His Word and Spirit.[2]

> A Christian doctrine of man is thus basic to any program of Christian education. A program that operates with something less than or other than a Christian understanding of persons is likely to produce something less than or other than Christian persons. The starting point for a Christian in his definition of true humanity is Jesus Christ. He is, for us, not only the revelation of the nature of God but also the revelation of the nature of man. To be human in our relationships with other people is to be mastered, as Jesus was, by a love that overcomes self and penetrates the misery of the other man. . . .

> The new man in Christ, of whom Paul speaks, is . . . simply man as God intends him to be. . . . God, who has come into our humanity in Jesus Christ, comes now actually into *my* humanity, so that He dwells in me as in a temple and by His Word and Spirit determines all things in my existence. . . . This is what man was created to be when God made him in His likeness. . . . Christ's work of redemption was a work of restoration, restoring to man the nature that God intended should be his from the beginning. . . .

113

> If God made man in His own likeness, then something has hap-
> pened to frustrate the design of God and to pervert man's nature.
> The answer of the Scriptures and of the Christian faith is that man
> sinned against God; lured by the prospect of being his own god,
> he defied the will of God. . . . Sin, therefore . . . is a proud self-
> centeredness which both alienates a man from God and disrupts
> his relationships with his fellow men.[3]

Thus, Christian growth is a matter of a person's relationship with God, with himself, his environment, and his fellow man. Maturity comes as a person moves out from self and grows to have harmony with the Center of his life, with that which he was meant to be—his real self, with God's created world around him, and with other people. Clarice Bowman says this sort of growth comes

> from an inner centering upon One who is all-wise, all-loving,
> from Whom radiate all the thoughts and actions of life. This is at-
> one-ment; for when one is in harmony inwardly with God, he is at
> one also with mankind and with the physical universe and with
> his own self. 'At-one-ment' is a good word. At the very mainspring
> of life is sure faith in God, belief that His ways are good ways
> and His purposes abounding in all-encompassing love.[4]

Such growth demands full participation on our part. It means being actively involved in the creative process, developing and using our resources, abilities, and talents as fully as we can in harmony with God's will for our lives. It is through the creative process—the giving of ourselves in further development—that we move from being just persons into the realm of becoming personalities.

No life moves through such development without difficulty, and yet it is precisely at the point of overcoming difficulties that the greatest growth often takes place. We are challenged beyond our known selves to draw upon those potentialities we never knew we had. With Junior Highs every experience in overcoming the challenge of difficulty fortifies them that much toward facing positively and maturely the difficulties that will threaten them later in life. The understanding counselor will seek to maintain such a rapport with his group and such a climate of love among them that no camper will feel the compulsion to keep his status in the group by making excuses to cover up his apparent failure. To a Christian this is even more meaningful because most of our difficulties are due to human sin and our growth as Christians depends to a great extent on our attitudes as we face the matter of sin. While our campers need to grow in their awareness of their own willful self-centeredness that disrupts their harmony with God and with other people, they also need to understand that they are still children of God, that God continues to love them in spite of their sinfulness, and is still

114

working within them to draw them into deeper fellowship with Him. A sense of vital fellowship with God is experienced perhaps most vividly as we feel sorry for our specific sinfulness, seek God's forgiveness, try to become reconciled with those with whom we are living, and in real humbleness yield our will to His.

One of the hardest things in life is learning to seek forgiveness, to say "I'm sorry" when I have wronged someone. A leader may be making the greatest contribution to a Junior High's life when he can help him overcome stubborn pride and say "I'm sorry" for the little things so that he can begin to experience the deeper meaning of forgiveness and reconciliation. We also need to help the campers realize that God loves us even in our sin, and that in the true Christian fellowship a person is loved for what he is and for what he can become through God, in spite of his present mistakes and sin.

Junior Highs are sensitive about their failures and suffer painfully over what they feel are their shortcomings. We cannot gloss over these feelings and be fair with them. It is probably true that boys and girls of this age do not understand the meaning of evil and suffering (do we?) but they are beginning to feel the depth of their impact, and their growth as Christians may be directly dependent upon these beginning encounters with God in the fellowship of the small camp group through realizing that their own insufficiency can be met by God's sufficiency.

Small group camping provides a new situation in which to develop a climate of Christian understanding and happy relationships conducive to real growth. To borrow a phrase from the Overstreets, the counselor needs to be a "space-making personality,"[5] one who seeks to provide room for each camper to be himself with sufficient freedom to grow in Christian grace. This means giving a camper sufficient room to "walk around a problem and look at it from new angles."[6] It means providing an openly friendly situation so a camper feels free to relax his defenses because they are no longer necessary for his acceptance in the group. Junior Highs who feel keenly the need to move out into new areas of activity and at the same time feel their sense of security threatened by what is new, can be helped to find sufficient security in their small camp fellowship and sufficient freedom in it to experiment in new endeavors. Each person to grow as a personality needs to gain self-respect by finding his own way around in life without being overly indulged or protected, and this is as true of growth as a Christian as in anything else. A camper needs opportunities to feel his own way in problems of faith through actual encounters with God, with His world, and with people, providing him with firsthand religious experiences. Christian faith means next to nothing when it is merely being outwardly pious and

115

proper, and repeating words of faith that have been handed down through the years. Jesus says to us much as He did to Peter and the other disciples, "But who do YOU say that I am?" God uses every experience of our lives, constantly confronting us with the revelation of Himself in His world, in Christ, in the Bible, and in His Spirit working through other people.

Christian growth then is made up of these deeper learnings that can take place through the intimate, everyday activities of small group camping. In each of these three areas of emphasis for Junior High camping, many of the same camping activities are carried on, the choice of them largely dependent upon the interests of the specific group of campers involved, with the opportunities of learning guided here by the counselor into a deeper consciousness of what is involved in growing as Christians. Small group camping offers the *means* by which Christian growth can take place through activities that involve accepting responsibilities; the handling of difficulties, disappointments, and differences of opinion; common sharing in fun, fellowship, and worship; group discussions; and time for the camper to be alone. Our purposes for this emphasis on Christian growth center in the following:

1. To provide opportunities for the camper to experience personal encounters with God so he can grow in his relationship with God and in his understanding of God's will for his life.
2. To provide opportunities for Christian growth in the camper's relationships with people.
3. To help the camper understand himself—his unique abilities and limitations—and to help him come to a sense of his destiny as a child of God.

Ways of Achieving These Purposes Through Camp Activities

In activities such as the following there are inherent opportunities for growth. But no leader should try to push for specific responses. If we have any faith in God we will simply try to open doors through which our campers may encounter God, and then step aside so as not to intrude on them in their personal experience with God who has His own way to each individual heart.

A. *To provide opportunities for a camper to experience personal encounters with God so he can grow in his relationship with God and in his understanding of God's purpose for his life.*

1. *Through contact with the things of our physical universe—God's world*

116

We can help campers relate God to His universe through such activities as the following:

(1) *Exploration and Discovery*

Discovery of the magnitude of God's creation, from such things as the tiny living organisms in the soil to the towering grandeur of the mountains; from the discovery through a field lens of the order and design of the scales on a butterfly's wing or the minute design hidden away in the heart of a flower, to the worlds beyond ours that glow in the starry heavens at night. Such discoveries lead naturally to expressions of wonder and appreciation, and a pause of simple, sincere thanksgiving in prayer helps to heighten a group's, and an individual's, awareness of God in His world.

Discoveries of the interdependence of all of plant and animal life reveal the wisdom and planning of God, reveal aspects of man's interdependence with the other parts of God's creation, and increase our awareness of man's responsibility in using these things.

Discovery of the story of the ages told in rock strata and in fossils and the shorter history told by tree stumps confronts us with the realization of how short our life span is in the eyes of God and often makes us feel humble in comparison.

The realization that God's creative processes are still going on in the world comes through observing such things as:

—the effects of erosion, especially after a rain.
—rivers gradually altering their courses or cutting new ones.
  the effects of the elements in their continual wearing down of
      mountains.
—a young growth of pines taking over an abandoned field.
—deeper in the forest the hardwood trees shade out the sun-loving
      pines in the struggle for survival.

Evidences of new life and new growth are seen everywhere around us. And God is still creating—in and through each of us! What a sense of oneness with the universal creative process, and with God! It leads to such questions as: What does God want us to do with our lives? How do we learn His will for us?

A discovery of death in nature—a bird, an animal—or the observation of conflict to the death among animals gives rise to many questionings on the part of campers. Here is a real opportunity to lead them into a personal awareness of God's plan for life and death; of the ongoing of life after death even in nature, as the decaying elements of the lifeless body contribute to the life-giving qualities of the soil; to a trust in God's love which promises life after death through Christ. We may

117

be afraid of death because it is an unknown experience and each person goes it alone, but a feeling of trust in God's love for us can be strengthened in us as we observe God's love in all other areas of life.

> To find design and harmony, balance and order, in nature is restorative to the souls of all who chafe under the disorder of the world's busy rush. Why is it restorative? Because something within seems to respond to the discovery of order.[7]

(2) *Times alone with God in His world*

Jesus found it restorative to go apart into the hills or out into the wilderness to be alone with His heavenly Father. Camp can provide just such experiences for campers to go apart, to think and watch and pray by themselves. In camps where a "morning watch" is observed, campers grow in their desire and ability to use such times alone with God in His world. In a very fine article, "Meet God Out-of-Doors," L. B. Hazzard says such times "readjust our values . . . help us to *center down . . . ,* giving us a sense of the wholeness of life. . . . 'The voice of the Lord is upon the waters'; 'The earth is his, and he made it' . . . —all these correct our disordered perspective and keep our fevered lives in the divine context. . . . Closeness to the natural universe *makes God real* as few experiences do."[8]

(3) *Sleep-outs* lead naturally to a feeling of dependence upon God and trust in His care for us. It is hard for one not to feel a deeper sense of oneness with the earth—quite literally and yet quite spiritually too!— lying on the ground in bedroll or sleeping bag, and God seems so much closer as one scans the heavens before falling asleep.

(4) *Star-Gazes* awaken an utter awe before the incomprehensible vastness of the universe. Almost unsought come the words of Psalm 8, "When I consider thy heavens . . . what is man, that thou art mindful of him?" Moments of worship come naturally and spontaneously.

2. *Through the Bible*

The Bible is a means of bringing God directly into our life. God is revealed in the Bible in the way in which He has dealt with men in Biblical history and He is also revealed as our God who seeks after us so that we may live according to His will for us. At times specific passages of Scripture will speak directly to a current situation in the life of the group or to an individual camper. At other times a whole book, or the sweep of the revelation of God through the whole of the Bible, will bear even more directly on the lives of our campers. God has been seeking to reveal Himself and His will for men—seeking to win men back from self-centeredness to the wholeness of life centered in Him—from the first chapters of Genesis to the end of the Biblical account, and even to each of us living here now!

So many of our boys and girls have been brought up on a "cafeteria" approach to the Bible in which they have referred to a bit of Scripture here and a bit there relevant to the specific lesson they have been studying. They have completely missed meeting or knowing the God who has been working in the lives of men and women throughout human history and who is revealed to us in the Bible.

One group of Junior Highs actually "discovered" Jesus in a vitally personal way when each of them sat down and individually read the book of Mark straight through. It all started when one boy said, "But Jesus doesn't seem real to me. Oh, I know all about His life, but I just don't feel as if I *know* Him." The group discussed the ways in which you get to know a person and the ways in which they thought they might get to know Jesus better. One idea was to read straight through one of the Gospels and let it tell its story just as they would let any other book tell its story. Then during the course of the next few days each one in the group took time to read the book of Mark through, since it was the shortest of the Gospels. Their reactions were startling. One girl said, "For the first time in my life I cried when I read the Bible—at the end of the story in Mark. It was so real I felt as if I were right there."

Too often we are apologetic about using Scripture passages of any length, and yet our boys and girls are used to covering ground in books at school and they gain more by digging into material than by dipping in. If we are to take the Bible seriously we need to really use it.

When specific passages are used in relation to a particular situation or problem we can help our Junior Highs get at the deeper implications of the Scripture by asking: What does this mean? How can we apply this in our lives? Or more specifically: How do you learn to love an enemy? What can we do to try to make a friend of someone who is mean to us? What is involved in forgiving? A counselor's advance consideration of the background and meaning of the "Helpful Scripture Passages" in this section will stand him in good stead when the need arises.

3. *Through prayer and worship*

(1) *Planned periods of individual and/or corporate worship*

Individual

Morning watch in a quiet place alone with God for meditation, Bible reading and other devotional reading if desired, and prayer. Encourage campers to take time to think their own thoughts after God instead of using the whole time to read, and suggest they write down ideas or prayers.

119

Times during the day when the group decides to separate for personal worship.

Bedtime devotional opportunities.

Corporate

Small group vespers and vespers with larger camp groups. Vespers can be planned by a committee within the small group for sharing with the rest of the group, planned by a small group for sharing with a larger camp vesper group, or each small group contributing its part to a larger camp vesper service.

Special services such as dedication services, Sunday worship, evening worship at a campfire, or other such worship experiences. Sometimes these will be solely for the small camp group and other times with the larger camp fellowship.

(2) *Spontaneous times of worship in response to a group's unfolding awareness of God.*

Moments of thanksgiving and praise at a particular aspect of beauty, wonder, and joy in God's world; i.e., joy in discovering a spring of cold water on a hike, wonder at the delicate beauty of fossil plants, the breath-taking beauty of a view from a hilltop, wonder on a star-gaze, or thanksgiving for a refreshing rain after a hot dry spell. Hymns, prayer, or appropriate Scripture may be used.

Times of prayer for guidance when the group is faced with some difficult problem or decision.

Times of prayer for forgiveness and the guidance of God's spirit of love when dissension has hurt the group.

4. *Through the use of creative activities*

Writing—poetry, prayers, litanies, ideas; drawing and painting; planning a dramatization for worship, etc. These activities provide an opportunity to clarify ideas or express an awareness of God, and at the same time such endeavor often leads to a growth in understanding God's will. We also need to encourage our campers to express themselves in worship—really participate with their own ideas and reactions—instead of depending too much on the words and responses of others.

5. *Through fellowship with others of the Body of Christ*

It is through our human experiences of love, in the giving and receiving of personality, that we first begin to comprehend God's love for us. In camp our sense of belonging to God is deepened through our active fellowship with others in the small group, in essence a part of the

120

Body of Christ. It is surprising how many campers find their first real experience of being wholeheartedly loved and wanted in their small group in camp. To youngsters who have been denied a warm, loving relationship at home, such a camp experience may be the most illuminating of their life. All the activities of camp—exploration and discovery, worship, discussion, playing and working together—that strengthen this sense of fellowship with others are also a means of helping us grow in our relationship with God and of deepening our understanding of God's will for our lives. Such activities in fellowship with others can lead us to new understandings and awarenesses through which we may encounter God.

B. *To provide opportunities for Christian growth in our relationships with people.*

1. *Through the small group fellowship*

The happy relationship with other campers in the small group in all their activities of camping—discovery, work, worship, and play—provides the climate in which a camper is stimulated to bring out the best in himself. In this new group he often feels free to try new attitudes of behavior which contribute to his growth as a Christian:

> —of being co-operative because his contribution is needed and appreciated;
> —of expressing his best ideas in the give-and-take of group discussion where he and others consider ideas objectively for what they are worth;
> —of growing in self-discipline through a real concern for the others in the group whom he has come to love;
> —of trying to be honest with himself, with God, and with his group because he senses that his place in the group and the love of others for him will not be threatened by admissions of failure on his part, but rather that by their loving support he will be strengthened to do better;
> —of giving himself in worship, prayer, and an expression of his deeper "religious" feelings in this avowedly Christian fellowship where such attitudes are accepted and expected.

Such experiences fortify the Junior High and give him a new frame of reference and a backlog of experience for use when he returns to the everyday world at home. Later a youth may be able to take a Christian stand because of such a group experience. He desires the approval of those he has loved and known in camp who bolster that which he feels is God's way for him, giving him moral support and enabling him to stand fast when others urge a lesser course of action.

Group activities themselves build character when they have a useful

121

purpose, require skill and effort to carry out, bring a sense of satisfaction in completion, and develop co-operation and a sense of belonging in the process.

(See list of activities which stimulate the growth of fellowship, under "Ways of Achieving These Purposes Through Camp Activities," in chapter on "Christian Community.")

2. *Through consciously seeking Christ's way in group life*

Camping provides a laboratory for Christian living which cannot be duplicated elsewhere in the life of the church. Christ and His principles become the point of reference as the group seek to make their daily life together more Christian.

> In discussions and planning we can ask such things as: What would Jesus do if He were in our place? How might He handle this problem? What might be some of Jesus' concerns in making this decision? Where have we failed? How could we have done better? Thus, the Bible becomes a necessary revelation of "the way" as a group seeks to be more Christian in its life.

> Prayer and worship were a natural part of Christ's life, and camp is a good place in which to let them become a more natural part of our everyday lives.

3. *Through a loving concern for others*

Where program develops out of the interests of the campers involved, campers are more able to lose their self-consciousness in a giving of themselves to what they are doing and to those with whom they are enjoying their activity. Friendship grows out of such mutually enjoyable activities and leads to a genuine concern for one another on the part of the campers. This can lead to real growth in their understanding of other people, a deeper sensitivity to the needs and desires of others, and experience in forgiving and accepting forgiveness. Very often initial attitudes toward campers change as greater understanding takes place, and campers come to realize their truer personalities. This concern for others is stimulated through all the camping activities. From the planning of activities and the sharing of experiences to "bearing one another's burdens" and "overcoming evil with good," discussions deepen our understanding of others, fun together is a natural expression of souls at one with God and man, and prayer undergirds our outgoing expressions of loving concern. (See brief illustration, "Each for All," in resource section of "Christian Community.")

122

4. *Through learning to see the best in others*

When Jesus looked at a person He saw not only his shortcomings but He saw deeper into the potential for good, for life as God wills it, that is within every person no matter how much it may be obscured by sin. No man is all bad, and no man is all good. Jesus, by seeing that good in man, was able to confront the individual with his potential for good, enabling the person to bring out the best in himself. Junior Highs can be helped to look for the good qualities in others instead of always seeing their weaknesses. A mature person doesn't feel the need of belittling others in order to make himself seem better by comparison, but rather he knows that looking for the best in others, seeing their potential for good and encountering the person on those terms, usually brings out the very best in both of them. This is an attitude toward life that campers can become aware of first, perhaps, when it comes up in discussion—a counselor may need to suggest it, for instance, when a group or individual is faced with a personality problem in a camper— and that can then be actively practiced when a group catches itself belittling or making fun of another camper or group.

5. *Through learning to assume responsibility for the group welfare*

The welfare of the small group depends upon each camper doing his share, taking his part, and accepting his responsibilities. If he fails both he and the group suffer. To help a camper grow in his ability to carry out responsibilities, a counselor will avoid the mistake many parents make of doing the job themselves to get it done. The camper with a tendency toward laziness needs to be put in situations in which he must act or he and the group will suffer; i.e., forgetting to bring the lemonade refreshment for their hike. Such a camper may need a suggestion or two to help him along but usually he will grow in his ability to respond if he feels his job is really a responsible one. In other words, campers respond if they feel the worth and need of assuming responsibility, and small group camping in which campers in large measure determine their own program, provides vital opportunities for campers to grow in their ability to handle responsibility. Dimock and Hendry, after carefully correlating camper activity and character growth, made this observation: "Every decision made by the counselor or adult in the situation literally robs the camper of an opportunity for learning. Each decision in which the camper shares contributes to his growth. Group projects seem to succeed in the degree that they challenge the full capacity of the campers to purpose, plan, execute and finally judge the product of their enterprise, and as they lead on to wider and wider interests and relationships."[9]

6. *Through consideration of the minority viewpoint*

In the democratic procedure of small group camping the individual finds himself a participating and therefore a controlling element, but he also discovers that in order to have others respect his point of view he must be a respecter of theirs. Each individual, unique in his ability and personality, is thus respected as much as a larger minority viewpoint. Sometimes in a desire to express their Christian love and concern, a majority will bend its will to that of the minority who could not wholeheartedly go along with the majority decision. Such struggling to effect the right and most Christian decision provides an experience in real growth.

One small group had planned a trip and a sleep-out when an invitation came to them to share in a progressive dinner with another group. There were conflicts in scheduling in both groups, and it was the minority opinion in the group receiving the invitation that the group should accept the invitation and sleep out at their campsite instead of on the trip as the majority wished. Finally the majority gave in and accepted the compromise offered by the minority. In a later evaluation they felt the trip sleep-out would have been a selfish decision and they were glad they had gotten better acquainted with the other group, had seen the other campsite and shared their own, and had had a sleep-out as well.

C. *To help the camper begin to understand himself—his abilities and limitations—and to help him arrive at a sense of his destiny as a child of God.*

1. *Discovering his own ability*

In small group camping the camper is given an opportunity to be a person in his own right, free from parental control and in a situation that provides sufficient security, through the friendliness of the small group and its leaders, to encourage each camper to contribute his best to the group life. What he contributes in ideas, activities, and evaluations is accepted if it is an honest expression of himself, and in being accepted he becomes involved in purposes and activities that draw on and develop his own inner resources. A camper discovers his "best self" when he seeks to give his very best to a group whose appreciation and approval he values—to be worthy of those he loves and who express love for him. Everything done in camp can be a means of fulfilling this purpose.

> Exploration and discovery bring to light new ideas, challenge the mind, encourage the searching out of information, and stimulate concern for sharing with the group.

Service projects, camp chores, cook-outs, and campcraft help a camper to develop his ability to plan and carry out responsibilities and give him the satisfaction of a job well done, besides providing the opportunity to learn the new skills that are involved and to increase his ability to work with people.

Worship experiences stimulate real participation in worship, increase a camper's ability to plan and conduct worship services and to grow in his capacity to worship.

Discussion and evaluations help a camper to grow in his ability to clarify ideas, weigh values, consider the other person's viewpoint, evaluate activities, and think objectively about problems in life. "One of the finest things about camping in small groups is that it enables each member to make the maximum number of decisions in matters affecting himself and his group."[10]

Creative activities give a camper an opportunity to try his hand and to develop his ability to use various creative media. (See Part II, chapter 4.)

Play times become real opportunities for being outgoing, sharing fun together, and learning new leisure-time skills such as swimming, boating, songs, games, etc.

Companionship with his counselor often leads a camper to identification with him and the principles for which he stands.

In camp there is freedom and time to experiment with new media and ideas, and this helps a camper discover more about his abilities and interests.

2. *Learning to accept his limitations and overcome his mistakes*

This is a very important aspect of achieving a mature sense of at-one-ment with ourselves. Each one of us has his unique combination of abilities and limitations, and young people need to be encouraged to discover and accept their limitations as much as they need encouragement in the development of their abilities. No one is happy in life trying to be what he is not and cannot be. Happy social experiences —being accepted as a contributing member of the group even if that contribution is simply being loving and co-operative—give a person a sense of security from which no lack of special ability will detract. We can help our campers realize that the important thing is to do the best we know how in any given situation, doing a job—any job—as we would for God our Father. Then our sense of limitation loses its importance. D. L. Moody hit at the matter adroitly when he said, "Let God have your life; He can do more with it than you can." We can help our campers overcome their dwarfing sense of limitation by:

Remembering to show appreciation for their efforts.

Encouraging a camper to keep at a task, to try just a bit harder, to accomplish a little more, to attempt something new.

125

Avoiding the easy way of depending on those campers we know can perform—giving others an opportunity.

Trying to get behind to the deeper meaning of a camper's excuses, to help him reach the point where he won't need them. The shy person, the arrogant, the bully, the youth who's been made to feel he's no good and won't try, the self-centered young person, the pessimist, etc., need our special attention.

Then there is the matter of being able to forgive ourselves for our mistakes, of learning the art of freeing the present and the future from the burdens of the past. If campers feel accepted by their counselor and by their group they will be more able to be honest about their mistakes, and will not feel as much need for defending themselves through assorted excuses, or putting the blame on the other fellow, or through rationalization. In a small group a camper who trusts his counselor and likes his group (and his place in it) can be helped to admit mistakes and learn to put them behind him as finished business through seeking the forgiveness of those he has wronged and, if necessary, through making amends for them. A counselor can help a camper by talking the difficulty over with him privately, and, if he wishes, by agreeing to help him express his feelings to the group by bringing the matter up in a pow-wow or other discussion time. A counselor may need to be prepared to guide the group if a discussion of the matter should follow and to lead in prayer as a means of closing the issue.

True forgiveness must be healing and the whole group can be helped to realize that there is as much art in being able to forgive as in seeking forgiveness. The person who forgives needs to realize "that the person who has faced his own mistake has, in the process, had to face himself as the maker of that mistake; and that this encounter with a painfully unflattering self-image may have left him raw on the edges."[11] To feel self-righteous about forgiving is not forgiving. A group can be helped to grow through their handling of friction and misunderstanding in their group, through discussions, through relevant Bible study, and through prayer.

Quite often in camp a group is faced with a problem camper, a youth so starved for affection that he has a negative outlook on life and a negative attitude toward people. How can a counselor lead a group to help such a difficult camper—or want to help him? Junior Highs fortunately tend to face life optimistically, and a group of campers can be tremendously optimistic about their ability to help a camper when they realize that even though it's hard to be kind and loving to such a person, that's exactly what is needed.

126

In one group there was a boy who was what the group described as "impossible." Intellectually he was far ahead of the others in the group and he reacted negatively to every approach to make him a part of the group. He enjoyed explorations and opportunities to spout off his knowledge but in no other way could one say he was a participant. However, the group and his counselor continued to seek to make him a part of the group by specifically asking his help in activities and discussions, although perhaps with less enthusiasm toward the end of the camp. After one of the final evaluation discussions the boy summoned enough courage to pray for forgiveness, "for being selfish . . . for being afraid to help . . . for making fun of others . . . for being too proud and smart . . . because I thought I was too good for them."

Campers can be helped to seek the forgiveness of those they have hurt by seeking first God's forgiveness. This helps to give one a sense of support and a sense that he is not alone in carrying out a difficult task.

3. Growing in his ability to handle time alone

Individuals need time alone so that they can understand themselves better. Some time should be provided in camp each day in which campers can be by themselves, to think, to relax and take in the beauties of the world about them, or to work on projects of their own—research, creative activities, or letter writing. Campers can grow in their ability to use time alone creatively if given the opportunity and suggestions on how to use it wisely and enjoyably. Counselors may profitably discuss with their groups the need for time to be alone and what each camper can do with such opportunities. Truly these pauses are ones that refresh and add vigor to corporate activities. Such times alone need not be scheduled for the small group as a whole. Sensitive counselors will be alert to times when individuals, or a group of campers, may benefit by time alone and thus make room for it. Very often the latter half of a siesta hour can be used, or times shortly before a meal in the dining hall when the group has no set-up duties there, or immediately after the evening meal in camp.

4. Growing in ability to handle responsibility

"In any democratic operation which places value on the 'growth of persons,' people must be entrusted always with more responsibility than they are at the moment fitted by experience to bear, as a condition of their development."[12] Junior Highs can often plan together well, but need help in carrying out the responsibilities they set for themselves. However, a counselor can help most, not by carrying on where they fail (washing the forgotten pots and pans at the campsite, gathering the forgotten firewood), but by encouraging them to finish a task, or by simply leaving it undone. Campers learn more about the need for assuming responsibility by returning to a campsite with dirty pots to clean before they can use them again, or missing out on a campfire because there was no wood gathered. Here is a pertinent opportunity for a discussion of the problem of responsibility and what it means to individuals and to groups. A counselor could lead his group by asking questions like: Who suffers when a person fails to be responsible? What does such irresponsibility do to the person who failed, or to the group who suffers? How can we learn to work together as Christians? How can we improve or help others improve? Such a discussion capitalizes on the group's unhappy experience and perhaps next time their experience will push their sense of responsibility further. Counselors can often do a job faster and better than their campers, but campers will never grow with a counselor who takes over for them nor with one who bosses them every step of the way. They will accept encouragement and suggestions from a companion counselor working with them.

Sometimes a counselor can help a camper grow in his ability to handle responsibility by creating a situation calculated to produce results—i.e., create a situation in which a lazy, unco-operative camper has to do his share or suffer the displeasure of the group. In some cases campers who seem immune to others' displeasure in his failures, can be somewhat changed by words of appreciation for even the little, almost insignificant, things that he does do.

Self-discipline also grows out of a camper's sense of responsibility toward the welfare of the group and his identification with the group as one of them. His own place in the group becomes more valued and important than his own selfish desires, and motivates his behavior accordingly.

5. *Understanding God's purpose for his life—coming to a sense of his destiny as a child of God*

When a camper begins to sense something of God's plan for His creation through contact with the things of the physical universe and has experienced joy in the fellowship of those who are seeking to be Christian in their lives, he comes to a point of imperative consideration: "What is *my* place in God's plan? Why am I here? What shall I do with *my* life?"

128

Helpful Scripture Passages

1. Knowing God and His Will

Through the Created World and Praise for It

Psalm 8—When I consider thy heavens . . .
        19—The heavens declare the glory of God.
      104—Psalm of Creation.
       95—O come, let us sing.
       96—Sing unto the Lord a new song.
     100—Make a joyful noise unto the Lord.

Through Prayer

Matthew 6:1-15—Jesus speaks of prayer. (The Lord's Prayer.)
Mark 1:35—Jesus prays alone.
Matthew 14:23—Jesus prays alone.
Luke 4:1-13—Jesus' temptation in the wilderness.
Luke 22:39-46—Jesus' prayer in Gethsemane.

Through God's Forgiveness

Matthew 6:12—Forgive us our debts.
Matthew 18:21-22—How often shall we forgive?
Matthew 18:23-35—The parable of the Unfaithful Steward, who
    wanted his debts forgiven but refused to forgive the debts
    others owed him.
Luke 23:33-34—Jesus on the cross. "Father, forgive them,"
Luke 15—Includes the parables of the Lost Sheep, the Lost Coin,
    and the Prodigal Son.
Luke 7:36-50—The sinful woman forgiven,
Luke 19:1-10—Zacchaeus is forgiven.
Luke 23:39-43—Man crucified with Jesus is forgiven.
Acts 26:9-19—Paul speaks of his changed life.
II Samuel 12:1-9, 13—David sins and is forgiven.
Psalm 51—David's prayer for forgiveness.

Through God's Will

Exodus 20:3-17—The Ten Commandments.
Matthew 22:37-40—The two great commandments.
John 14:6-15—Jesus reveals the Father and His will.
Matthew 5:1-16—The Beatitudes.
Matthew 13:18-23—The parable of the Sower.
Matthew 19:16-22—The rich young ruler.
Hebrews 11:1—12:2—Now faith is the assurance of things hoped
    for. (May be used 11:1-10 and 12:1-2.)

Through Men Who Knew God's Will for Them

Abraham—Genesis 12:1-9; 13:14-18; 22:1-18.
Moses—Begins in Exodus 3 (especially Exodus 3:1-12, and 20:1-17.
    The Ten Commandments).
Samuel—I Samuel 3:1-21.
David anointed to be king—I Samuel 16:1-13.
Isaiah—Isaiah 6:1-9.
Paul—Acts 9:1-31.

129

2. Growing in Relationship with Others

Planning and Working Together

Romans 12—One body with many members.

Matthew 7:1-5—Judge not, that ye be not judged.

Colossians 3:12-17—Serving others—Jesus washing the disciples' feet.

John 15:12-17—Love one another.

Handling Conflict and Difficulty

Matthew 5:38-48—Love your enemies.

Matthew 5:21-24—Be reconciled with your brother.

Romans 12:14-21—Overcome evil with good.

Galatians 6:1-2—Bear one another's burdens.

I Peter 3:8-17—Accept criticism.

I John 2:9-11—Rid your heart of hate.

(See additional Scripture references on pages 77-78.)

3. Living as a Child of God

Developing Our Abilities

I Corinthians 3:16-17—You are a temple of the Holy Spirit.

Matthew 25:14-30—The parable of the Talents. (We must make use of the abilities God has given us or we will lose them.)

I Corinthians 12:4-31—Having different gifts, use them.

I Corinthians 13—The greatest of these is love.

Accepting Responsibility

Moses and his struggle to accept responsibility

Exodus 3:1-10—God speaks to Moses in the burning bush

3:11—Moses is afraid to do God's will

3:12—God replies

4:1, 10-15—Moses' excuses and God's replies

4:17-21—Moses assumes his responsibility

Nehemiah accepts the responsibility of rebuilding the walls of Jerusalem—Nehemiah 1 and 2

Jeremiah couldn't believe the Lord had chosen him to be a prophet—Jeremiah 1:4-10

Jonah fled from doing God's will—Jonah 1:1-3
but finally did it—Jonah 2:10—3:3a

Jesus in Gethsemane—Luke 22:39-46, especially verse 42

Living According to God's Will

John 15:1-11—The vine and the branches.

John 15:12-17—Friendship with Jesus.

Matthew 25:31-46—As you did it to one of the least of these . . . you did it to me.

John 3:16-21—Eternal life.

Philippians 3:12-16—Forgetting what lies behind . . . I press on toward the goal.

The book of James and the book of I John could be used in their entirety as advice to Christians.

Hymns for Christian Growth Emphasis

Make Me a Captive, Lord
God, Who Touchest Earth with Beauty
Breathe on Me, Breath of God
Spirit of God
Once to Every Man and Nation
Take My Life, and Let It Be
I Would Be True
O Jesus, I Have Promised
Jesus Calls Us
Dear Lord and Father of Mankind
That Cause Can Neither Be Lost Nor Stayed
Be Thou My Vision
O Master, Let Me Walk with Thee
Lord, I Want to Be a Christian
Evening Star
Have Thine Own Way, Lord
My Jesus, As Thou Wilt
Give of Your Best to the Master
"Are Ye Able," said the Master
Open My Eyes, That I May See
Lord, Speak to Me

Resources in Prose and Poetry

BRIEF ILLUSTRATIONS

The Accusing Fingers

The late Peter Marshall once said, "Every time I point one finger of accusation at someone else, I find three other fingers pointing at myself."

The Master of the Devil[1]

The story is told of an old man who was being examined for membership in the church. On being asked if he had mastery of the Devil he replied, "I'se got de Master of de Debbil."

—R. A. Lapsley, Jr.

The Parable of the Trees

1. Trees grow a little new wood every year and it is on the new wood that the blooms and fruit appear.
2. Trees have a large root system for support and their roots go deep for the life-giving water.
3. Trees give as they get.
    They take in carbon dioxide through their leaves and give off oxygen needed by men and animals.

131

As they take water from the earth they use only a small part (2%) of it themselves and give the rest back into the air through their leaves.

4. Trees are amazingly adaptable to their environment and have wonderful powers to overcome injuries to them.

5. Trees live to bear fruit.

Prayer Paths[2]

Armin Oldsen has reminded us of a Christian mission in West Africa where the native converts were taught to spend time each day speaking with God in private. In time a path would be worn from the convert's hut to the prayer spot in the brush. Failure to use the path regularly would result in an overgrown prayer path. The sight of an overgrown prayer path would prompt fellow members to admonish the backslider with the words: "Brother, there is something the matter with your prayer path." Such an admonition is needed by many people today and would, if heeded, forestall many spiritual tragedies.

—A. Gordon Nasby

Great Personalities Who Overcame Difficulty[3]

Helen Keller—Blind and deaf from an early childhood disease she was thus shut off from the world except for her senses of touch and smell. It took hard work and struggle for her to learn even to communicate with her teacher and friend, but she did learn to read and write and speak. She has devoted her life to promoting better care for the blind throughout the world.

Beethoven—One of the world's greatest musical geniuses, who became totally deaf and yet was able to transfer the superb music in his mind and heart onto paper for others to play and enjoy.

Franklin Roosevelt—He suffered crippling polio early in his career and yet he carried on with such vigor that many people seeing him for the first time were utterly shocked at how crippled he was.

Kagawa—The great Japanese Christian who has never been physically well at any time during his whole ministry to the poor, the outcasts, and the laborers of his native land.

George Washington Carver—A humble Negro scientist who never let the prejudice shown against him because of his race keep him from giving his best in making discoveries that have been a blessing to all mankind. His favorite Bible verse was Proverbs 3:6, "In all thy ways acknowledge him, and he shall direct thy paths."

We could name others—Robert Louis Stevenson, weak and sickly all of his life; Marian Anderson, who suffered prejudice against her because she is a Negro; and Abraham Lincoln, who grew up in a very poor home.

Or that humble Christian woman in one of our smaller churches, who, inwardly eaten up with cancer, was able to show a

132

radiant, joyous spirit to everyone. Her minister often said he never went to her house to bring her strength and comfort but that he came away greatly refreshed and strengthened himself. Even on the day she died, she summoned the strength to bake pies for her family "to leave them something to enjoy."

—John and Ruth Ensign

POETRY

Attainment[4]

Use all your hidden forces. Do not miss
The purpose of this life, and do not wait
For circumstance to mold or change your fate.
In your own self lies destiny. Let this
Vast truth cast out all fear, all prejudice,
All hesitation. Know that you are great,
Great with divinity. So dominate
Environment, and enter into bliss.—

Love largely and hate nothing. Hold no aim
That does not chord with universal good.
Hear what the voices of the silence say,
All joys are yours if you put forth your claim;
Once let the spiritual laws be understood,
Material things must answer and obey.

—Ella Wheeler Wilcox

The Winds of Fate[5]

One ship drives east and another drives west
With the selfsame winds that blow.
'Tis the set of the sails
And not the gales
Which tells them the way to go.

Like the winds of the sea are the ways of fate,
As we voyage along through life:
'Tis the set of a soul
That decides its goal,
And not the calm or the strife.

—Ella Wheeler Wilcox

The Cross at the Cross-ways[6]

See there!—God's signpost, standing at the ways
Which every man of his free-will must go,—
Up the steep hill,—or down the winding ways,—
One or the other every man must go.

He forces no man, each must choose his way,
And as he chooses so the end will be;
One went in front to point the Perfect Way,
Who follows fears not where the end will be.

133

To every man there openeth
A Way, and Ways, and a Way,
And the High Soul climbs the High Way,
And the Low Soul gropes the Low,
And in between on the misty flats,
The rest drift to and fro.
But to every man there openeth
A High Way and a Low,
And every man decideth
The Way his soul shall go.
                                    —John Oxenham

The World's Bible[7]

Christ has no hands but our hands
    To do His work to-day,
He has no feet but our feet
    To lead men in His way,
He has no tongue but our tongues
    To tell men how He died,
He has no help but our help
    To bring them to His side.

We are the only Bible
    The careless world will read,
We are the sinner's gospel,
    We are the scoffer's creed,
We are the Lord's last message,
    Given in deed and word.
What if the type is crooked?
    What if the print is blurred?

What if our hands are busy
    With other work than His?
What if our feet are walking
    Where sin's allurement is?
What if our tongues are speaking
    Of things His lips would spurn?
How can we hope to help Him
    And hasten His return?
            —Annie Johnson Flint. Copyright. Re-
            produced by permission. Evangelical
            Publishers, Toronto, Canada.

STORIES

Parable of the Builders[8]

Once upon a time there was a certain rich man who had it in
his heart to do good. One day, as he was walking out over his
broad estate, he came to a little house down in a hollow where
lived a man with a very large family. Upon inquiry, the good rich

134

man learned that he who lived in the little house was a carpenter, a builder of other people's houses, while he and his family had to live in this little hovel in the hollow. The rich man thought long upon it, then he sent for the carpenter and put before him the plans of a beautiful house and said, "I want you to build me a house just like this over on that sunny hill," and he pointed out one of the loveliest building places in all the neighborhood. "I want you to build it good and strong," he said. "Employ only the best workmen and use only the best materials, for I want it to be a good house." Then he went away on a long journey and left it all to the builder. After the rich man had gone the carpenter said to himself, "This is my chance. Other men have made more than wages with an opportunity like this." So he skimped the material and skimped the labor and covered the house over with paint so nobody could see how very poorly it was built. At length the rich man returned and the carpenter brought him the keys and said, "This is a fine house I built for you over on the sunny hill." "Good!" said the rich man, and he handed the keys back to the builder. "I am glad it is a good house. I have intended all along to give it to you when it was finished. The house is yours."

The builder was thunderstruck. How industriously he had been cheating himself when he thought he was cheating his neighbor! He took the keys and walked away and muttered to himself again and again, "Oh, if only I had known that I was building the house for myself!"

—Edwin Markham

The Strongest Wood[9]

I remember going up a mountain path one day when I met a mountaineer with an ax in his hand. We were so high that there were few large trees above us; only rocks, a sparse growth of craggy and gnarled bushes and stunted trees, and the immensity of the blue sky above. As we were going the same way I walked with him, and eventually asked him what he was going to cut.

"I need a piece of timber to fix my timber wagon," he said. "You know that does the heaviest and most rackingest kind of work, and the tree that grows on the top, where the storms hit it hardest, is the tree that has the toughest wood. If ever you want to get a piece of timber to stand all the jolts and strains, cut it from a place where all its life it has been obliged to stand the same kind of roughness. A tree that ain't shielded," he said, "is the last one to fall. It has stood so much in the way of storms, little by little, that when the big gale comes, it can weather it."

—Archibald Rutledge

His Bread Tasted Sweet[10]

If you had been passing the St. John's Catholic Church in the steel town of Aliquippa, Pennsylvania, one day in the spring of 1939, you would have seen crowds of people, seven hundred or of them, going inside. The cars in front of the church would have told you that it was a funeral that had brought such throngs of people there.

"What a very important person it must be to have so many people going to his funeral!" you would have thought. "It must be the mayor, or the president of the largest bank, or a famous explorer, or perhaps the richest man in town."

If you were curious enough, you might have asked someone, "Whose funeral?"

"Mario Ezzo's," the answer would have been.

"But who is Mario Ezzo?" you might well have asked.

The answer would have surprised you. "He's the shabby little old man who was always cleaning the streets."

After such a strange answer, you would have made a business of finding out why so many people were honoring a shabby old street cleaner. And this is what you would have learned.

Seven years before, Mario Ezzo had left Italy to make his home in America. This country was good to him, and he learned to love it. He still loved Italy, but there was room in his loyal old heart for the love of two countries. He was glad of work to do, even though his wages were so small that he could not lay aside much money for the time when there might be no way for him to earn, for the time when his feet would be less quick and his arms less strong.

The time finally came when no one seemed to need his help. He went from place to place, looking for work, but there were enough younger men to do all the work for which there was money to be paid. Finally, there was nothing for him to do but to tell the men who gave out relief money that he, Mario Ezzo, could find no way to earn. When the relief agents looked at the little old man, they did not hesitate to put him on the relief rolls. He was so shabby and so wizened that they were sure he must be very poor. They wondered why he had not come to them sooner.

"Here are three dollars and sixty cents," said the relief agent. "Come each week and you will receive the same amount."

Mario thanked him and went away.

Now so far this story is just like the story of hundreds and thousands of other people. But here comes the part that is different. Some men would have grumbled because three dollars and sixty cents a week is such a wee amount of money. They would have wondered how the government expected them to live on so little. They would have been sure that never again would they do any harder work than bringing a loaf of bread home from the bakery.

That was not Mario's way. When he thanked the relief agent, he really meant that he was grateful. When people are really grateful, they think of some way to show it. The first thing that Mario did when he left the relief office was to get a huge stiff brush. Then he went out into the dirtiest street he could find and began to sweep. He swept and he swept. Six days of the week and eight hours of the day, Mario Ezzo could be found sweeping the streets of Aliquippa. Each day he worked, rain or shine, and was seen at different times going beyond the town limits to repair sewers and dig surface water drains. He whistled as he worked, for he was a happy man. Why should he not be? He had work to do for others.

"Why do you work so hard?" people would ask him. "You get your relief money without working. Why bother to work?"

And Mario would stop whistling long enough to give an answer in English that was hard to understand. Italian was so much easier for him to speak. "I think this is a wonderful country," he would say. "I decide I will be an honest man with this country. They give me money to live. So I keep this town clean like table. It makes my bread taste sweeter. I am a man because I work." Then Mario Ezzo would bend to his work again, sweeping and sweeping as he whistled old Italian melodies.

This was the little old street cleaner whose funeral was packing the church. The people of Aliquippa, most of them steelworkers, later erected a monument for this man who worked for others so humbly, yet so usefully. The inscription on the stone reads, "Work makes me feel good inside. My bread it tastes sweet."

—Alice Geer Kelsey

The Second Mile[11]

The great road that stretched for miles in both directions was crowded. Groups of people on foot traveled steadily onward. Donkeys, heavy-burdened, passed along. A long train of camels with great bulky loads high on their backs plodded by.

The boy David, standing by the side of the road, watched everything with eager eyes.

"Some day I'll follow the road on and on and on," he thought. "I'll follow it down to the Great Sea—and I'll not stop even there!"

His eyes fell upon a single figure, walking alone along the crowded road. "He's a Roman soldier," thought David. "I can tell by the way he's dressed. How I hate the Romans! If it weren't for them we Jews would be free again. Then we shouldn't have to pay their taxes! Or obey their laws! I hate them all!"

He stared at the Roman soldier who was almost opposite him now in the road. Suddenly the soldier stopped. He shifted the heavy pack he carried and eased it down to the ground. Then he straightened up again and stood resting a moment, watching the people passing by.

David still stared at him, thinking angry thoughts. Then just as the soldier turned to pick up his pack once more he noticed David standing not far off.

"Here, boy," he called. "Come here!"

David wanted to turn and run but he did not dare. No one dared to disobey one of the soldiers of Rome. David went nearer, slowly. The soldier motioned to his pack. "You will carry it for me," he said.

137

Now David knew well that there was no help for it. He knew the hated Roman law. Any Roman soldier could make any Jewish boy or man carry his load for him in any direction he was traveling, for one mile.

"But only for one mile!" thought David, angrily, as he picked up the pack.

The soldier had already turned away and started on along the road. He did not even bother to look back to see that David was following him. He knew he would not dare do anything else.

David followed. The pack was heavy but David was strong. He swung along easily but his thoughts were angry. He wanted to throw the soldier's pack down in the dirt and stamp on it. He wanted to shout and rage at that hated Roman soldier striding easily ahead of him. But he could do nothing except follow along, keeping his bitter thoughts to himself.

"Well, it's only a mile," he thought, "just one mile. He can't make me go a step farther. Only one mile."

The words made a sort of song in his mind in time to his steps. "One—mile; one—mile."

Then as he was plodding along David suddenly remembered another day when he had walked along this same road. He had gone out a little way from the city with some of his friends to find a young teacher of whom they had heard. They had found him out on the hillside among a crowd of people. David had stopped with the others to listen to what he said.

"What made me think of him now?" wondered David with one part of his mind. Another part was still repeating over and over, "One—mile; one—mile."

"Of course," he remembered suddenly. "The Master used those very words. What was it he said about one mile?" He walked on, frowning, for a moment before he could remember. Then he said the words to himself. " 'Whosoever shall compel thee to go one mile, go with him two.' That was what he said!" David had not paid very much attention to it at the time. He remembered now other things the Master had said. " 'Love your enemies.' 'Do good to them that hate you.' " Then once more David found himself repeating the strangest of them all. " 'Whosoever shall compel thee to go one mile, go with him two.' Does he mean—could he mean—like—now?" David puzzled. "But why? Why should I go more than one mile?"

David was so busy thinking that he did not notice that the soldier had stopped, and so he almost ran into him.

"You have come a mile," said the soldier. "Give me the pack."

"I will go on," said David. And he did not know why he said it. "It has not seemed far. I am not tired."

The Roman stared at him in surprise, and for the first time David really looked into his face. He saw that the soldier was very young. He saw too that he was very, very tired, in spite of the straight, soldierly way in which he stood

"You have come a long way," said David

138

"Yes," said the other, "a weary way of many miles."

"Have you far to go?"

"I go to Rome."

"So far!" said David. "Then let me carry your pack another mile. There is no one here to take it. Another mile will be nothing."

"You are very kind," said the soldier, and his face was still full of surprise.

So they went on, only now the Roman waited for David and walked beside him along the road. And suddenly David found himself talking to the soldier as if they had known each other for a long time. He told him all about his home and family. He listened while the soldier talked of his travels in far places. They were so busy talking that the distance seemed short.

"Tell me," said the soldier at last, "how did it happen that you offered to come this second mile?"

David hesitated. "I hardly know," he said. "It must have been something the Master said, I think." Then he told the soldier all that had happened out on the hill and all that he could remember of the Master's teachings.

"Strange!" said the soldier thoughtfully. " 'Love your enemies.' That is a hard teaching. I should like to know this Master."

They had come now to the top of a hill and to the end of the second mile. David looked back along the road toward his home. "I must go back," he said.

The soldier took his pack and shouldered it again. The two clasped hands. "Good-by . . . friend," said the soldier.

"Good-by . . . friend," answered David, smiling up into the soldier's eyes.

As David strode back along the road the words of the Master kept running through his mind: " 'Whosoever shall compel you to go one mile, go with him two.' " And as he repeated the words he found himself adding with a strange, deep joy: "It works! There's something in it! I walked one mile behind an enemy—I walked the second mile and found a friend!"

—Truman B. Douglass (adapted)

Part IV
COUNSELOR'S PLANNING SECTION

Suggestions for Planning Your Own Program

A SECTION is given here to help counselors plan their own program. All that is said in the rest of the book is of little value unless the counselor takes time to relate it to his own camp experience, to make it his own by using it. An informal program takes far more planning and advance preparation than a "canned" program. A counselor needs to know where he wants to go and why, and also to have an idea of the various ways in which a group can travel to get there. Or, to say it another way: "The benefits of relaxed informality and flexibility are possible only if undergirded by a strong sense of direction, reasonable limits, and a secure knowledge of possible courses of action."[1]

The counselor will need a notebook in which to expand this Planning Section as a means of developing his own program. These plans will be tentative, subject to further planning with his co-counselor, and with the campers themselves. The notebook could be divided into the following sections for further development:

    I. Your Group of Junior Highs
    II. Your Purposes for This Camp
    III. Possible Experiences as Means of Achieving These Purposes
    IV. Plans for Arrival of Campers and First Day Together
    V. Daily Plans
    VI. Plans for After-Camp Follow-up

I. Your Group of Junior Highs

Name
Age and school grade
Home situation

140

Brothers and sisters, older and younger?
Problems? Interests? Church?
What do parents want camp to do for camper?
Significant experiences and responses of camper during camp.

II. Your Purposes for This Camp

You will find special help in Part I and Part III of this book. Also consider your purposes with your co-counselor. Ask yourself:
What should happen to the campers?
In understanding?
Discover what?
Learn to do?
Experience together?

III. Possible Experiences as Means of Achieving These Purposes

This list of activities will include more than can possibly be used. The most important ones may be checked. You and your co-counselor can work these out with your own camp, its facilities and terrain, in mind. The actual choice and daily plan of activities will be worked out within your small group of campers. Part III of this book should give you plenty of suggestions of activities. Add your own. Be sure to include:
Activities
Exploration possibilities
Discussion ideas (Perhaps list resources—Scripture, stories, poems —you wish to use in relation to these discussion ideas.)
Worship possibilities (Include resources here too.)

IV. Plans for Arrival of Campers and First Day Together

These need to be worked out in advance. The section in this book on the arrival of campers, Part II, may help you plan with your co-counselor for this time. Be sure to list:
Ways of getting started
Things to do
Materials needed
Specific plan of activities

V. Daily Plans

These will be worked out according to blocks of time, including regularly scheduled things such as meals, rest hour, and bedtime, and allowing large spaces for activities which will be planned with the campers. A chart such as the Sample Camp Schedule for Small

141

SAMPLE CAMP SCHEDULE FOR SMALL GROUP

	Monday	Tuesday	Wednesday	Thursday	Friday	Saturday	Sunday
Rise Morning Watch	(Time)						
Breakfast 8:00			Cook-out				Cook-out
Morning		Clean up shelters and washhouse Fix pack-lunch Exploration hike	Family devotions Clean-up chores Planning activities at campsite Swim	Camp chores Campsite construction Cook-out planning Swim	Camp chores Fix pack-lunch Exploration hike	Camp chores Shelter construction for sleep-out Cook-out planning Swim	Family devotions Clean-up Discussion *Worship Service
Lunch 12:30		Pack-lunch			Pack-lunch		
Afternoon	Arrival Refreshments Make name tag Shelter group orientation Explore campsite	Rest after eating Exploration end at small group campsite Wood gathering Swim	Rest Campsite construction Swim	Rest Cook-out preparation Swim Cook-out in progress	Rest after eating Hike home Swim Small group games	Rest Sleep-out preparations continued Cook-out preparations Swim	Longer rest Compass hike to spot where picnic supper will be found
Supper 6:00				Cook-out		Cook-out	*Picnic
Evening	Small group get acquainted Games Discussion *Campfire	Vespers Pow-wow Review activities Make plans	Vespers Fun Campfire Songs, stories, games Refreshments Pow-wow	Vespers Pow-wow	Vespers Campfire with another small group Pow-wow	Vespers Pow-wow Sleep-out	*Vespers Return hike by trail *Campfire songs stories
Cabin Devotions	9:15 In shelter	In shelter	In shelter	In shelter	In shelter	Under stars	In shelter

142

* Total camp activities.

Second week add new activities. Plan special closing activities.

Group on page 142 is very helpful in developing daily plans for the camp period. You and your co-counselor may work out on such a chart your specific plans for the arrival of campers and your first day together, and then develop a tentative plan for the entire camp period. This, along with your listing of possible experiences under III in your notebook, will give you a good basis for guiding the thinking of your campers in the actual developing of your small group plans with them. Such a chart will also help them visualize their plans, and will of course be subject to extensive revision with them during the camp period.

VI. Plans for After-Camp Follow-up

This will include ideas of things to say in letters to campers and parents, planning with director and staff about follow-up with pastors, teachers, and church area groups (like Presbytery youth meetings or conclaves), and plans for visits or Christmas letters. See Part II, chapter 7, for help.

Bibliography

Small Group Library

Some camps find it helpful to provide a basic set of resource books to be kept at each small group campsite. The following might be a helpful list for such a small group library:

Your Own Book of Campcraft, Catherine T. Hammett. Pocket Books, Inc., New York, 1950.

Nature Lore Manual for Church Leaders, Reynold E. Carlson, The Methodist Publishing House, Nashville, Tenn., 1945.

The Web of Life, John H. Storer. A Signet Key Book, The New American Library, New York, 1953.

Golden Nature Guide Series. Simon and Schuster, New York.

  Birds, Herbert S. Zim and Ira N. Gabrielson.

  Flowers, A Guide to Familiar American Wildflowers, Herbert S. Zim and Alexander C. Martin.

  Stars, Herbert S. Zim and Robert H. Baker.

  Trees, Herbert S. Zim and Alexander C. Martin.

  Insects, Herbert S. Zim and Clarence Cottam.

  Weather, Paul E. Lehr, R. Will Burnett, Herbert S. Zim.

  Mammals, Herbert S. Zim, Donald F. Hoffmeister.

  Seashore, Herbert S. Zim, Lester Infle.

Altars Under the Sky, Dorothy Wells Pease. Abingdon-Cokesbury Press, New York, 1942.

American Folk Tales and Songs, Richard Chase. A Signet Key Book, The New American Library, New York, 1956.

General Camp Library

Church Camping Publications

International Journal of Religious Education, October 1956 issue, special issue on Church Camping. Order from National Council of Churches, Box 238, New York, N. Y.

International Journal of Religious Education, May 1957 issue, special issue on Christian Growth in Dynamic Groups.

Toward Better Church Camping, National Council of Churches, New York.

Administration

ACA Standards, American Camping Association, Martinsville, Indiana.

Administration of Group Work, L. H. Blumenthal. Association Press, New York, 1949.

Administration of the Modern Camp, Hedley S. Dimock (Editor). Association Press, 1950.

Camping in the Program of Christian Education. The National Council of Churches, New York, 1954. Leaflet describing the unique contributions which camping may make to the Christian education program.

The Book of Camping, Robert Rubin. Association Press.

Handbook of YMCA Camp Administration, edited by Ledlie and Roehm. Association Press.

Outdoor Hazards—Real and Fancied, Mary V. Hood. The Macmillan Co., 1955.

Counselor Training Programs

The Art of Group Discipline, Rudolph M. Wittenberg. Association Press, 1951.

Group Leadership and Democratic Action, F. S. Haiman. Houghton Mifflin Co., Boston, 1951.

Camp Counseling, A. Viola Mitchell and Ida Barksdale Crawford. W. B. Saunders, New York, 1950.

Counselor-In-Training Course, Camp Fire Girls, Inc. Department of Camping, Camp Fire Girls, Inc., 16 E. 48th Street, New York 17, N. Y.

So You Want to Help People, Rudolph M. Wittenberg. Association Press, 1947.

So You Want to Be a Camp Counselor, Elmer Ott. Association Press, 1951.

Talks to Counselors, Hedley S. Dimock and Taylor Statten. Association Press, 1947.

The Camp Counselor's Manual, Ledlie and Holbein. Association Press, New York, 1946.

Crafts and Campcraft

Book of Arts and Crafts, Marguerite Ickis and Reba Selden Esh. Association Press, 1953.

Campcraft ABC's, Catherine T. Hammett. Girl Scouts of U.S.A., New York.

Creative Crafts for Campers, Catherine T. Hammett and Carol M. Horrocks. Association Press, 1957.

Easy Crafts, Ellsworth Jaeger. The Macmillan Co., New York.

Jack-Knife Cookery, James Wilder. E. P. Dutton and Co., New York, 1923.

Nature Crafts, Ellsworth Jaeger. The Macmillan Co., 1947.

How to Make Pottery and Other Ceramic Ware, Muriel P. Turoff. Crown Publishers, New York, 1949.

144

Handicraft: Simplified Procedure and Projects, 9th ed., Lester Griswold. Prentice-Hall, Englewood Cliffs, N. J., 1953.

The Junior Book of Camping and Woodcraft, Bernard S. Mason. A. S. Barnes and Co., New York, 1943.

Use of Native Craft Materials, Margaret Shanklin. Charles A. Bennett Co., Inc., Peoria, Ill., 1948.

Nature Lore

Adventuring in Nature, Betty Price. Association Press, 1940.

The Amateur Naturalist's Handbook, Vinson Brown. Little Brown & Co., New York.

Audubon Nature Bulletins, National Audubon Society, New York, N. Y. 80 or more bulletins on various nature subjects.

Basic Science Education Series, Parker, Bough, etc. Row, Peterson and Co., Evanston, Ill., or White Plains, N. Y. More than 60 small booklets on nature.

A Beginner's Guide to Fresh Water Life, L. A. Hausman. G. P. Putnam Sons, New York, 1950.

Boys' Book of Snakes, Percy Morris. The Ronald Press, New York, 1948.

Evening Sky Star Charts, Hayden Planetarium, New York. Set of four charts, one for each season.

A Field Guide to the Birds, Roger Tory Peterson. Houghton Mifflin Co., 1947. Most extensive guide to birds.

A Field Guide to the Mammals, Burt and Grossenheider. Houghton Mifflin Co., 1951.

A Field Guide to the Shells of Our Atlantic and Gulf Coasts, P. A. Morris. Houghton Mifflin Co., 1948.

A Field Guide to the Western Birds, Roger Tory Peterson. Houghton Mifflin Co., 1941.

Handbook of Nature Study, A. B. Comstock. Cornell University Press, Ithaca, N. Y., 1948.

How Miracles Abound, Bertha Stevens. The Beacon Press, Inc., Boston, 1941.

How to Know the Trees, Harry E. Jaques. William C. Brown Co., Dubuque, Iowa, 1946.

Nature Games and Activities, Sylvia Cassell. Harper & Brothers, New York, 1956.

Rocks and Their Stories, Fenton and Fenton. Doubleday & Co., New York, 1951.

The Sea Around Us, Rachel L. Carson. Oxford University Press, New York, 1951.

Wild Flower Guide, Northeastern and Midland United States, Edgar T. Wherry. Doubleday & Co., Inc., 1948.

Worlds in the Sky, Fenton and Fenton. John Day Co., Inc., New York, 1950.

How to Know and Predict the Weather, R. M. Fisher. New American Library of World Literature, New York, 1953.

Worship

Meditations Under the Sky, Dorothy Wells Pease. Abingdon Press, 1957.

Altars Under the Sky, Dorothy Wells Pease. Abingdon-Cokesbury Press, New York, 1942.

How to Plan Informal Worship, Winnifred C. Wygal. Association Press, New York, 1955.

Services for the Open, L. I. Mattoon and H. D. Bragdon. Association Press.

Spiritual Values in Camping, Clarice M. Bowman. Association Press, 1954.

Treasury of American Indian Tales, Theodore Whitson Ressler. Association Press, 1957.

Twenty Tepee Tales, Marvin M. Lotz and Douglas Monahan. Association Press, 1950.

Worship Ways for Camp, Clarice M. Bowman. Association Press, 1955.

Storytelling and Campfire Programs

And Promenade All, Helen and Larry Eisenberg. Fun Books, New York, 1952.

Camp Fire and Council Ring Programs, Allan A. Macfarlan. Association Press, 1951.

Grandfather Tales, Richard Chase. Houghton Mifflin Co., 1948.

Just So Stories, Rudyard Kipling. Doubleday & Co.

The Jack Tales, Richard Chase. Houghton Mifflin Co., 1943.

The Handbook of Skits and Stunts, Helen and Larry Eisenberg. Association Press, 1953.

The Storyteller in Religious Education, Jeanette Perkins Brown. The Pilgrim Press, Boston, 1951.

Notes and Acknowledgments

Part I—Purposes and Preparation

Chapter 3. Preparation for Camp

1. From *Camping and Christian Growth* by Lynn and Campbell Loughmiller, p. 22. Copyright 1953. By permission of Abingdon Press.

Part II—Program Guidance

Chapter 3. Campcraft

1. John and Ruth Ensign, *Stewards in God's World*, pp. 122-123. (Slightly adapted.) Copyright, 1953, by John Knox Press, Richmond, Va. By permission.

2. *Ibid.*, pp. 115-117. (Adapted slightly and expanded.)

Chapter 4. Use of Creative Activities

1. Ensign, *Stewards in God's World*, p. 104.

2. *Ibid.*, pp. 123-127. (Slightly condensed.)

Chapter 5. Special Program Helps

1. Ensign, *Stewards in God's World*, pp. 58-59.

2. *Ibid.*, p. 82. (Adapted.)

3. Loughmiller, *Camping and Christian Growth*, p. 40.

4. *Ibid.*, p. 33.

5. Ensign, *op. cit.*, p. 88.

Part III—The Threefold Emphasis for Junior Camping

Emphasis 1. Christian Community

1. Nelle Morton, *Living Together as Christians*, pp. 37-38. Copyright 1952 by the Christian Education Press, Philadelphia. Used by permission.

2. Charles Stinnette, Jr., "Walk in the Spirit." Reprinted by permission from the February 1957 issue of *Pulpit Digest*. Copyright 1957 by the Pulpit Digest Publishing Company.

Emphasis 2. Christian Stewardship

(This chapter includes Chapter III of *Stewards in God's World* by John and Ruth Ensign, minus chapter title and several section titles, and slightly expanded.)

1. Alan Paton, *Cry, the Beloved Country*, pp. 3-4. Copyright 1948 by Alan Paton; used by permission of the publishers, Charles Scribner's Sons.
2. Fairfield Osborn, *Our Plundered Planet*, p. 193. Little, Brown & Company, 1948. By permission.
3. Carolyn W. Robinson, "Peace in Earth," in *Christian Herald*, June 1952. By permission.

Emphasis 3. Christian Growth
1. From *The Teaching Ministry of the Church* by James D. Smart, p. 162. Copyright, 1954, by W. L. Jenkins, The Westminster Press. Used by permission.
2. *Ibid.*, p. 167.
3. *Ibid.*, pp. 157-158.
4. Clarice M. Bowman, *Spiritual Values in Camping*, p. 83. Association Press, 1954. Used by permission.
5. Harry and Bonaro Overstreet, *The Mind Goes Forth*, p. 139. W. W. Norton & Company, Inc., New York, 1956. Used by permission.
6. *Ibid.*, p. 149.
7. Bowman, *op. cit.*, pp. 64-65.
8. Lowell B. Hazzard, "Meet God Out-of-Doors." Reprinted by permission from the November 1956 issue of the *International Journal of Religious Education*.
9. Hedley S. Dimock and Charles E. Hendry, *Camping and Character*, p. 80. Association Press, Second Edition, 1939. Used by permission.
10. Loughmiller, *Camping and Christian Growth*, p. 19.
11. Overstreet, *op. cit.*, p. 120.
12. Paul F. Douglass, *The Group Workshop Way in the Church*, pp. 95-96. Association Press, 1956. Used by permission.

Part IV—Counselor's Planning Section
1. From *God at Work in His World*, by Mary E. Venable, p. 40. Copyright, 1955. By permission of Abingdon Press.

Acknowledgments

RESOURCES IN PROSE AND POETRY

Christian Community
1. Ben Hecht, in *A Guide for the Bedevilled*. Copyright 1944 by Charles Scribner's Sons. Used by permission.
2. Dr. J. E. Kwegyir Aggrey, "Parable of the Piano." Quoted by Daniel Johnson Fleming in *Christian Symbols in a World Community*, p. 126. The Friendship Press, 1940. Used by permission.
3. L. B. Hazzard, "Each for All." Reprinted from *Spiritual Values in Camping* by Clarice M. Bowman, p. 149. Association Press, 1954. By permission.
4. Gossip Illustration adapted.
5. Mary Carolyn Davies, "A Prayer," in *The Hymnal for Youth*. Copyright, 1941, by The Westminster Press.
6. Thomas Curtis Clark, "The Search," in *The Hymnal for Youth*. Used by permission of Mrs. Thomas Curtis Clark.
7. Miriam Teichner, "Awareness," second stanza, in *Masterpieces of Religious Verse*. Copyright, 1948, by Harper and Brothers. By permission.

147

8. Thomas Curtis Clark, "God's Dreams," in *1000 Quotable Poems*. Copyright, 1937, by Willett, Clark & Company. Used by permission of Mrs. Thomas Curtis Clark.

9. Edwin Markham, "A Creed" (first stanza) and "Outwitted." Reprinted by permission of Virgil Markham.

10. Grace W. McGavran, "The Church That Was Builded by Moonlight," in *We Gather Together*. Friendship Press, 1941. Used by permission.

11. Frank Johnson Pippin, "The Fable of Heaven and Hell," in *Best Sermons 1949-50*, edited by G. Paul Butler. Harper and Brothers. By permission.

12. Leo Tolstoy, "Where Love Is." Retold from "Where Love Is, There God Is."

Christian Stewardship

1. Walter C. Lowdermilk, "Eleventh Commandment." Reprinted from bulletin issued by Soil Conservation Service, United States Department of Agriculture. By permission.

2. William L. Stidger, "Going to School to God." Copyright 1921 by Christian Century Foundation. Reprinted by permission from issue of June 9, 1921.

3. Alice Geer Kelsey, "The Clocks Stood Still." From *Stories for Junior Worship* by Alice Geer Kelsey. Copyright 1941 by Whitmore and Stone. By permission of Abingdon Press.

4. Leo Tolstoy, "How Much Land Does a Man Need?" (Adapted.)

Christian Growth

1. R. A. Lapsley, Jr., "The Master of the Devil," in *Portraits of the Master*. Published by Board of Women's Work, Presbyterian Church, U. S. (Adapted.)

2. A. Gordon Nasby, "Prayer Paths." Excerpt from "Let's Learn to Pray." Reprinted by permission from the January 1957 issue of *Pulpit Digest*. Copyright 1956 by the Pulpit Digest Publishing Company.

3. John and Ruth Ensign, "Great Personalities Who Overcame Difficulty." Adapted in part from material by John and Ruth Ensign in *Pioneer Bible Studies*, July-September, 1957, p. 16. Presbyterian Church, U. S. By permission.

4. Ella Wheeler Wilcox, "Attainment," in *1000 Quotable Poems* compiled by Thomas Curtis Clark. By permission of Estate of Thomas Curtis Clark.

5. Ella Wheeler Wilcox, "The Winds of Fate," in *Masterpieces of Religious Verse*. Harper & Brothers, 1948. By permission.

6. John Oxenham, "The Cross at the Cross-ways." From *Gentlemen—the King!* by John Oxenham. The Pilgrim Press. Used by permission.

7. Annie Johnson Flint, "The World's Bible," in *By the Way*. Used by permission of Evangelical Publishers, Toronto, Canada.

8. Edwin Markham, "Parable of the Builders." Reprinted by permission of Virgil Markham.

9. Archibald Rutledge, "The Strongest Wood." From *Peace in the Heart* by Archibald Rutledge. Copyright 1930 by Archibald Rutledge, reprinted by permission of Doubleday and Company, Inc.

10. Alice Geer Kelsey, "His Bread Tasted Sweet." From *Stories for Junior Worship* by Alice Geer Kelsey. Copyright, 1941, by Whitmore and Stone. By permission of Abingdon Press.

11. Truman B. Douglass, "The Second Mile." Adapted by Florence M. Taylor in *The Storyteller in Religious Education* by Jeanette Perkins Brown. Copyright, 1951, The Pilgrim Press. Used by permission.

Date Due